101 must-know ACOUSTIC LICKS

PLAYBACK+
Speed • Pitch • Balance • Loop

To access audio visit:
www.halleonard.com/mylibrary

Enter Code
3987-8383-7654-8710

ISBN 978-1-4234-6027-5

7777 W. Bluemound Rd. P.O. Box 13819 Milwaukee, WI 53213

In Australia Contact:
Hal Leonard Australia Pty. Ltd.
4 Lentara Court
Cheltenham, Victoria, 3192 Australia
Email: ausadmin@halleonard.com.au

Visit Hal Leonard Online at
www.halleonard.com

Preface

This special reference volume is designed for all unplugged guitarists. Arranged for quick, easy reference, it contains a wide range of stylistic phrases, commonly known as "licks" (those essential, self-contained instrumental figures tucked into your favorite compositions), utilized by the great artists we all admire.

Inside are 101 definitive licks from the acoustic guitar repertory, neatly organized into easy-to-use categories. They're all here: classical, blues, folk, rock, jazz, country, pop, and more. Browse to your heart's content and feel free to tap into the feeling of each lick that speaks to you. As you do, you take the vital first step of reinvention that connects you to the infinitely beautiful world of the unplugged masters.

—Wolf Marshall

Contents

Introduction

The acoustic guitar is ubiquitous in our culture and has been since early in the last century—and why not? There's nothing like making music on an unplugged guitar with just your hands. Its resonance has crossed numerous boundaries; it has merged genres, created new genres, and is now an integral part of many divergent styles. You'll find plenty of evidence for that assertion in this volume consisting of must-know licks in the subgenres of classical, blues, folk, rock, country, pop, and jazz. This book is a departure from previous works in the *101 Must-Know Licks* series. Whereas the others each addressed a particular style (such as blues, rock, and jazz), the focus here is on the myriad sounds and traditions of the acoustic guitar across boundaries and through the decades.

Guitar music is a language with a variety of dialects. Speaking on the guitar with authenticity and eloquence requires more than finger dexterity, a facile mind, or a creative impulse; it requires a sense of tradition and a seemingly endless well of ideas. In non-literary cultures, the act of communication and the art of conversation are learned through what is known linguistically as "oral tradition"—a tradition passed down from generation to generation by listening, imitating, mastering, and ultimately reinterpreting with personal expression. So it is with the music of the acoustic guitar.

The great acoustic guitar players throughout history have studied, absorbed, and repurposed the contributions of their forebears. Picture Jimi Hendrix repeating Tommy Johnson's rural blues licks until they are part of his vocabulary and flow naturally when he plays a tune like "Hear My Train A Comin'." Or imagine Chet Atkins struggling to get Merle Travis' fingerpicked polyphony under his fingers. And then consider the Travis/Atkins picking tradition in the music of subsequent virtuosos like Jerry Reed and Doyle Dykes. Virtually every classical guitarist—from Julian Bream to Christopher Parkening—memorized and reinterpreted Andrés Segovia's gut-string contributions to the form and continued in his footsteps. And neoclassical metallists Yngwie Malmsteen and Randy Rhoads tapped into the spirit of the Elizabethan lute masters, as well as the music of J.S. Bach and the baroque/classical tradition. In any case, the assimilation process largely entails the learning and mastery of specific phrases and techniques (akin to sentences in language), or *licks*. This can be a daunting task, considering the vast amount of musicians and styles across the genres.

Enter *101 Must-Know Acoustic Licks*: a handbook of essential phrases in a wide variety of styles and genres within the acoustic guitar world. Each lick is a self-contained phrase with a central idea or focal point and an indispensable piece of the acoustic guitar vocabulary. The 101 licks are presented in distinct segments within a larger genre, be it classical, pop, rock, blues, jazz, country, or folk. If you're already an acoustic guitar aficionado, this book may revive some delightful memories and inspire you to take your current playing down some familiar old paths. If you're coming to this guide with an interest that outweighs your knowledge of the genres, expect to be taken on a trip over the unplugged landscape, with a soundtrack to match, from which you will emerge a more knowledgeable, conversant, and passionate player.

Tips for Using This Book

1. Memorize these licks as soon as possible.
2. Master the technical requirements of each lick. These can vary from classical rest and free strokes to country/blues collapsed-wrist postures for Travis picking and muting, folk-strummed patterns, and intricate single-note melodies and arpeggiations.
3. Make notes, mental or written, about the feel of each lick. Your visceral, emotional reaction to a lick is part of the ad-lib selection process when improvising or applying. This process could involve forming a visual image of the lick's physical shape—how it sits on the fingerboard and how it relates to a particular chord form.
4. Add at least one new lick a week to your working vocabulary. Memorize and **use it** in your current musical situation—playing with a band, adding it to an existing solo or song arrangement, jamming with your friends, etc. Moreover, the performing acoustic solo player of the coffee house variety will be well-served to add the licks to his or her current and new repertory.
5. Capo users: play nut-position licks with open strings in various capoed positions on the fingerboard. You will notice that the timbre, string feel, tension, and fret distances have a bearing on how the lick feels. Note the key changes as you move the licks to different positions. Part of an acoustic picker's repertory includes a number of capoed tunes.

About the Audio

To access the audio tracks that accompany this book, simply go to **www.halleonard.com/mylibrary** and enter the code found on page 1. This will grant you instant access to every track, for streaming or download.

Each lick is played twice on the accompanying audio: first at the normal tempo, and then, after a brief pause, at a slower tempo.

Classical and Spanish

The catchall label "classical guitar" has been applied to the genre since its rise to prominence in the early years of the 20th century. The classical guitar repertory was established by a handful of innovative players and grew into a powerful art form. It is generally performed on a nylon-string instrument.

Classical guitar grew from humble beginnings in the 1600s as a Spanish descendant of the lute and Italian guitar. Important composers like Guiliani, Sor, Tárrega, Carcassi, Albéniz, Rodrigo, and Villa-Lobos wrote much of the body of traditional classical guitar music. Moreover, music from composers like J.S. Bach and Mozart was transcribed and adapted for guitar. Classical guitar was largely brought into the mainstream through the efforts of Spaniard Andrés Segovia and his protégés.

The classical guitar, once an obscure instrument, and its repertory have since crossed over to influence pop, rock, folk, and country styles. The effect can be heard in Steve Howe's Spanish guitar masterpiece "Mood for a Day," Rik Emmett's "Am Prelude," Randy Rhoads' character piece "Dee"—as well as his intros to "Diary of a Madman" (borrowed from Leo Brower) and "Revelation Mother Earth"—and Yngwie Malmsteen's Bach-inspired "Black Star." Classical guitar enjoyed pop success in the Top 40 realms with Mason Williams' instrumental hit "Classical Gas," a juxtaposition of light classical themes, Spanish modality, and folksy strumming over an orchestral backing.

Performance requirements for classical guitar are demanding and strict, even of a disciplined player. Technique involves specific coordination of the plucking fingers (*p* = thumb, *i* = index, *m* = middle, and *a* = ring) and a high level of expertise to articulate intricate arpeggiation, counterpoint, singing melodies, and varied chordal textures.

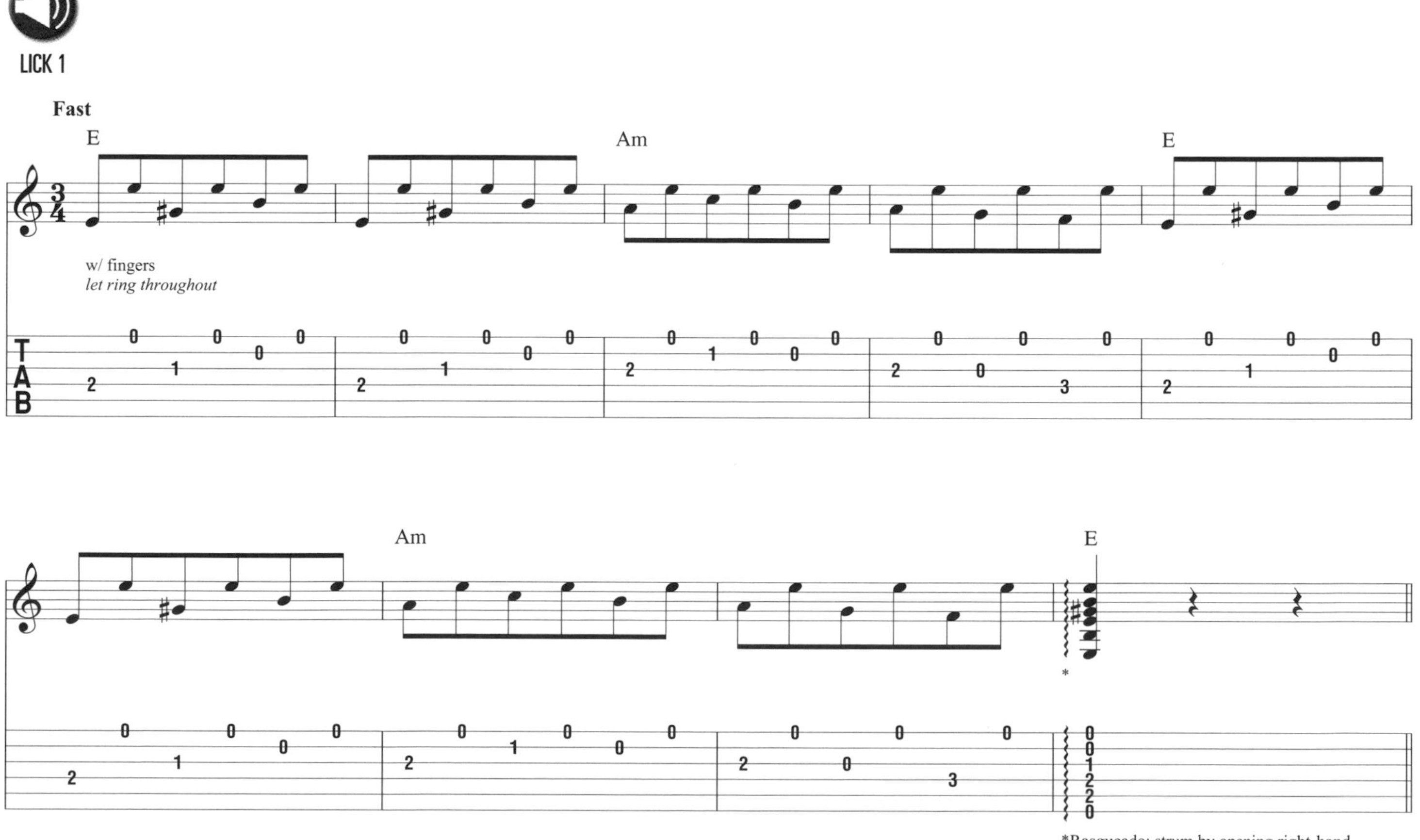

*Rasgueado: strum by opening right-hand fingers quickly and striking strings with nails.

LICK 2

Moderately
E
Am
Dm
E
w/ fingers

Am
Dm
E

LICK 3

Moderately
Em
w/ fingers
let ring throughout

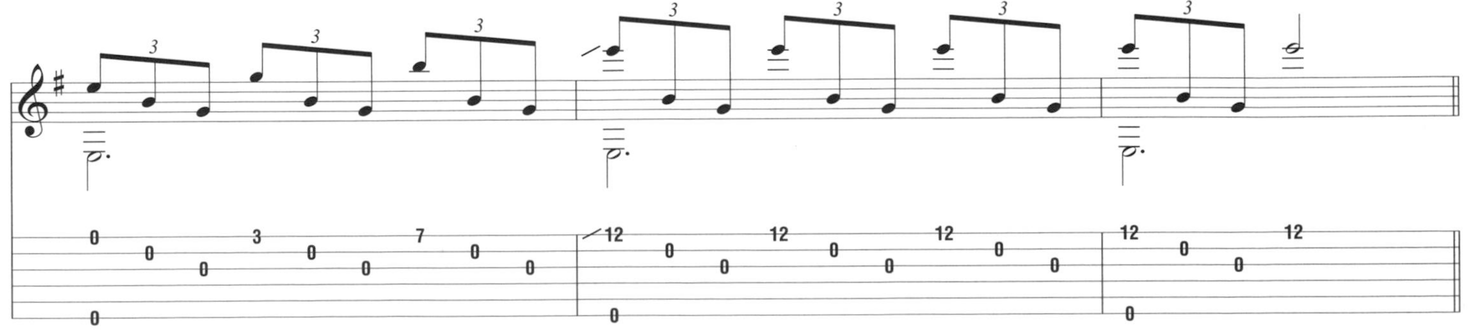

LICK 4

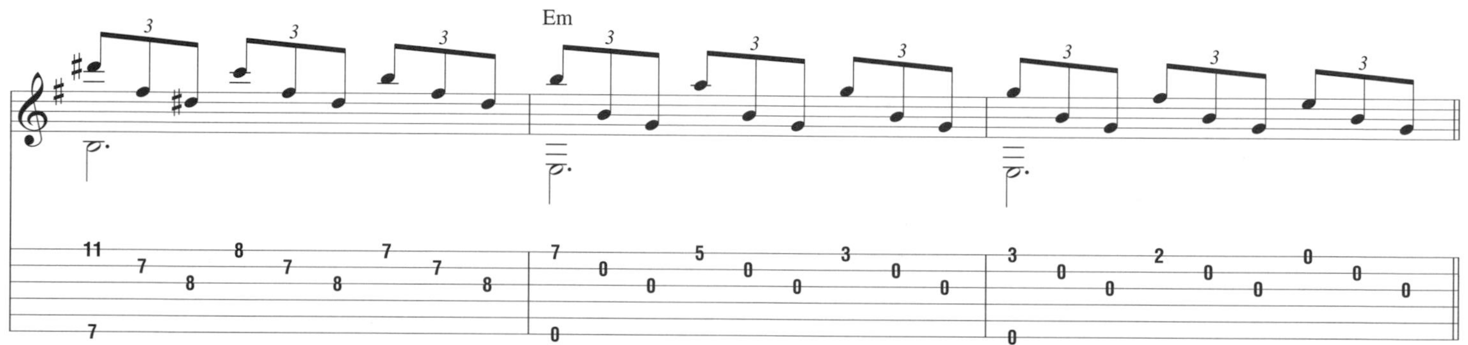

LICK 5

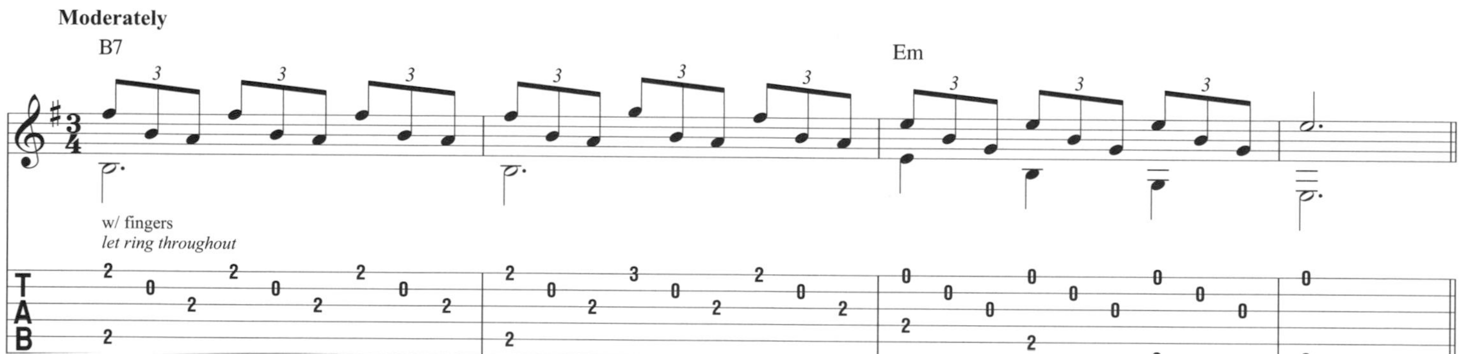

LICK 6

LICK 7

Moderately
Em
B7
Em/G
B/F♯
Em
D7/F♯
w/ fingers
TAB

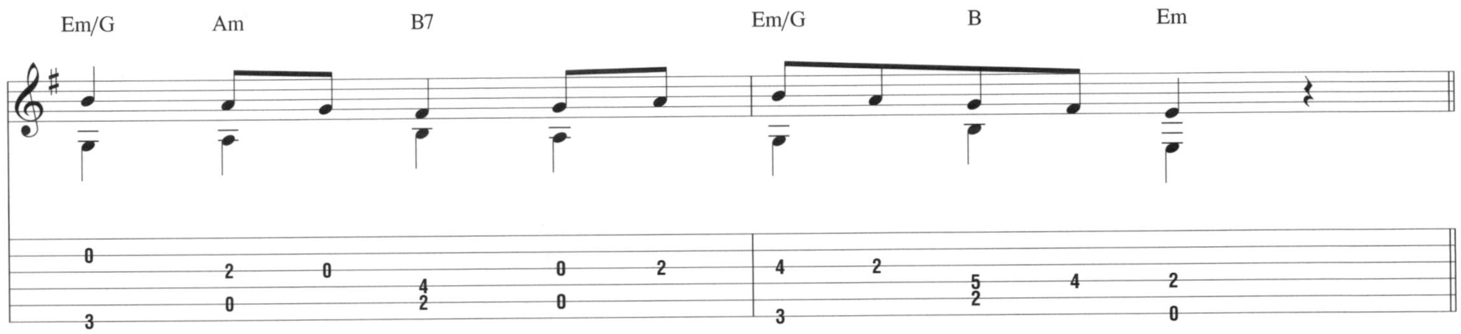
Em/G
Am
B7
Em/G
B
Em

LICK 8

Moderately slow

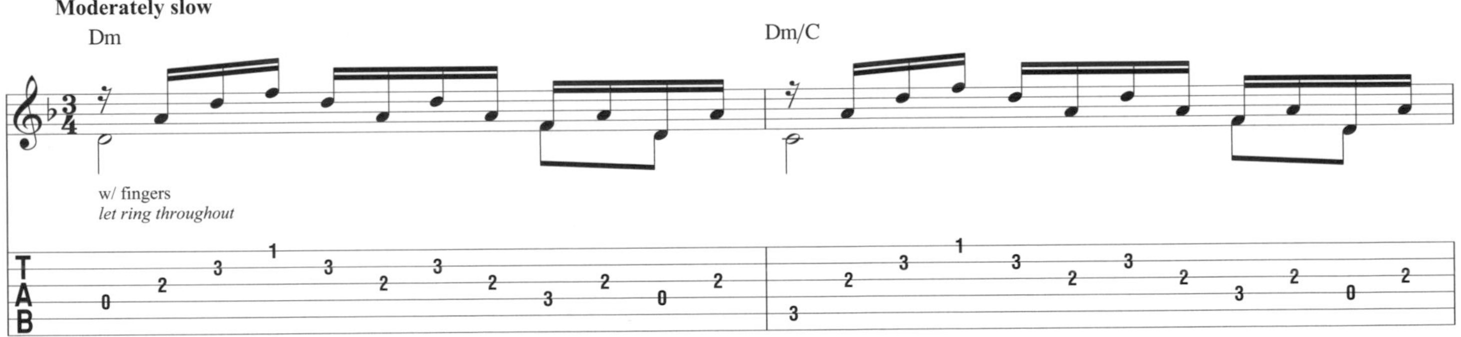
Dm
Dm/C
w/ fingers
let ring throughout
TAB

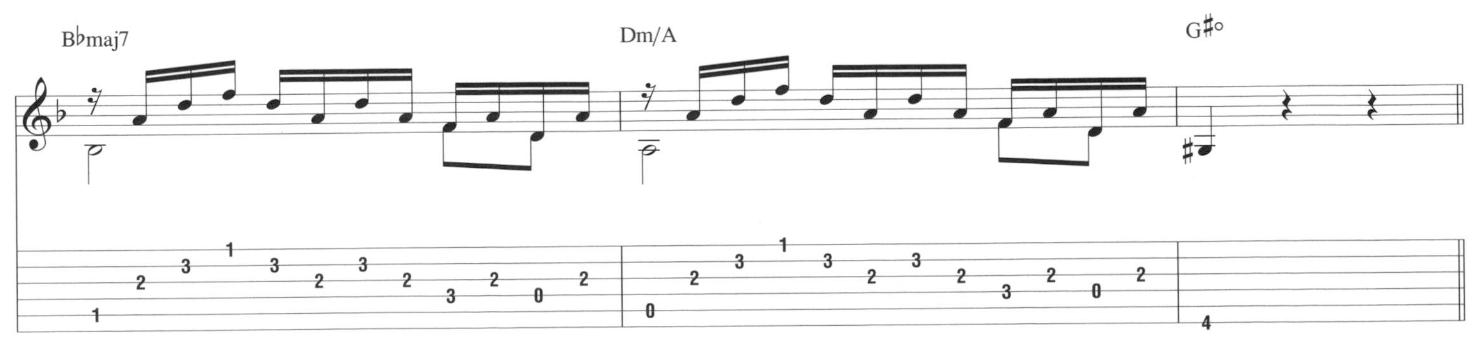
B♭maj7
Dm/A
G♯°

LICK 9

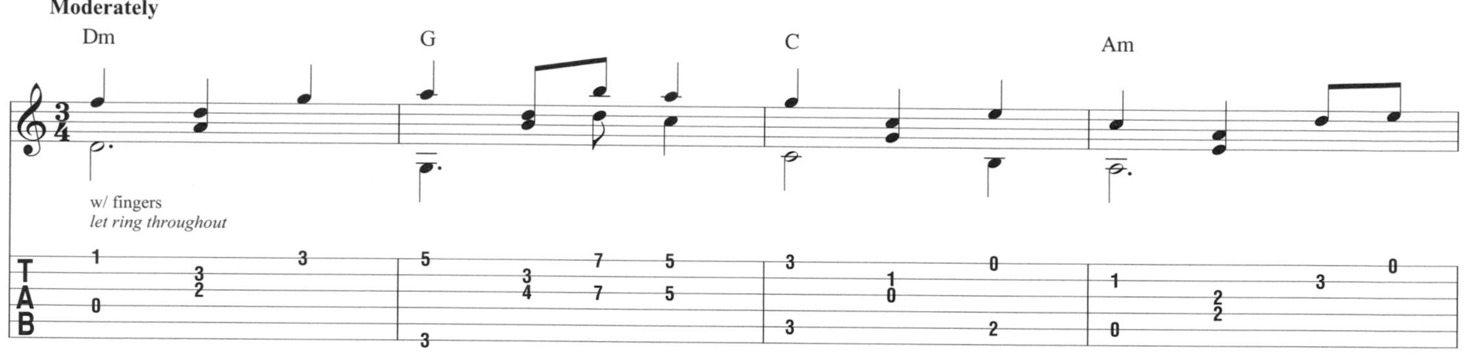
Moderately
Dm
G
C
Am
w/ fingers
let ring throughout

Dm
E7
Am
Am/G

LICK 10

Moderately
Dm
G
C
Am
w/ fingers
let ring throughout

Dm
Em
Dm/F
A7
Dm

LICK 11

LICK 12

LICK 13

LICK 14

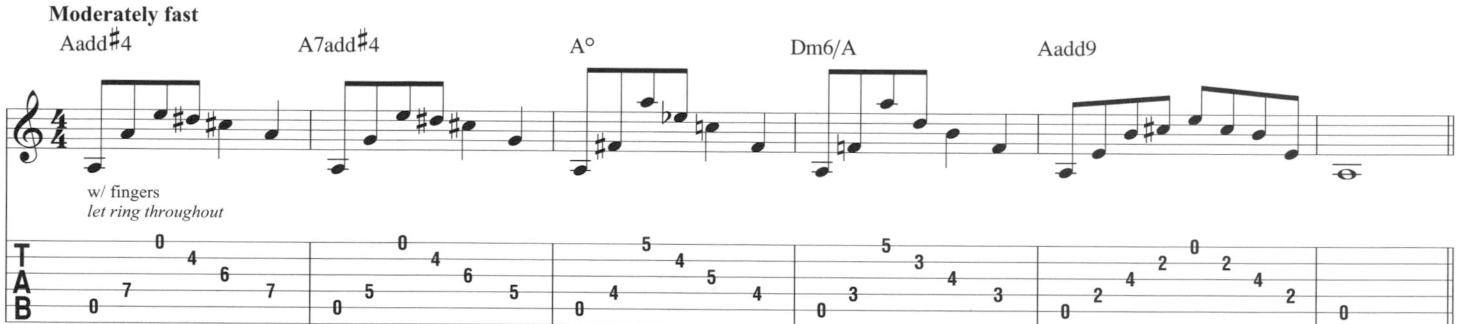

LICK 15

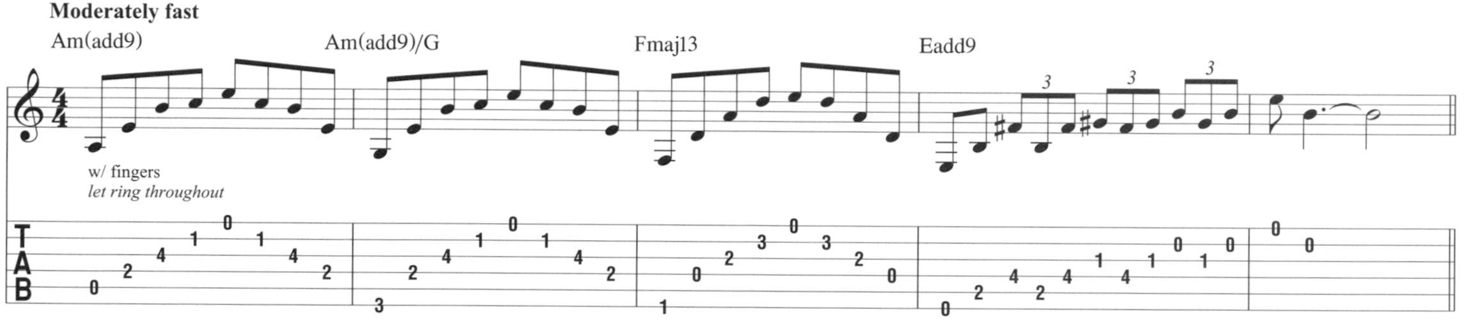

LICK 16

LICK 17

LICK 18

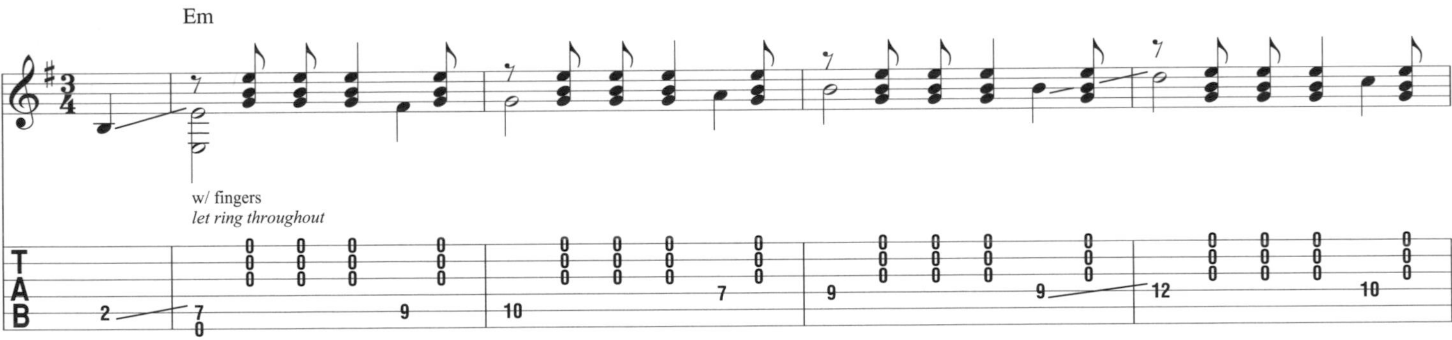

LICK 19

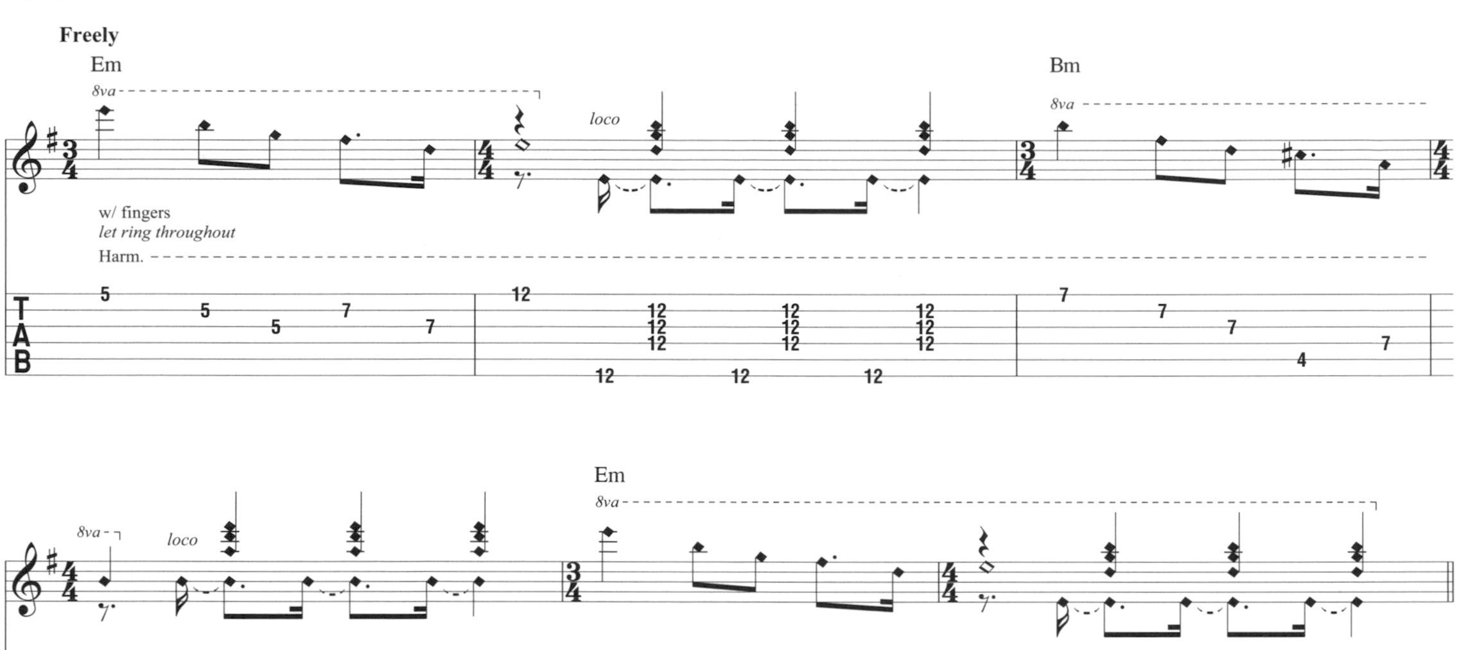

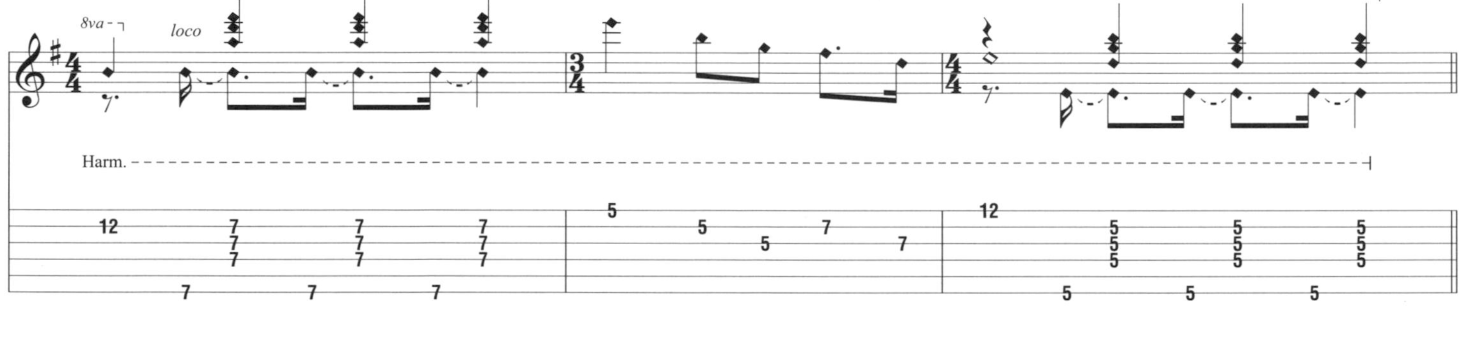

LICK 20

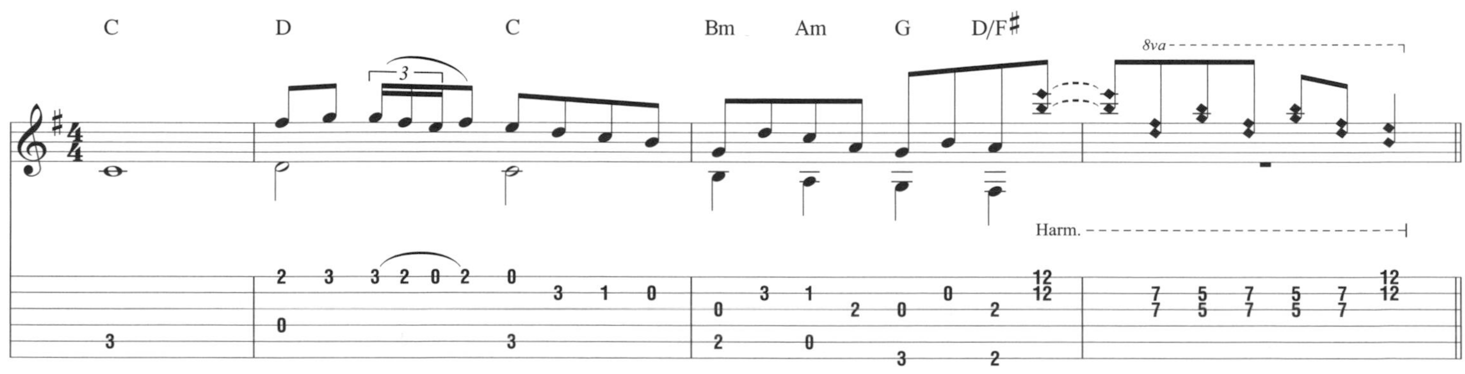

LICK 21

LICK 22

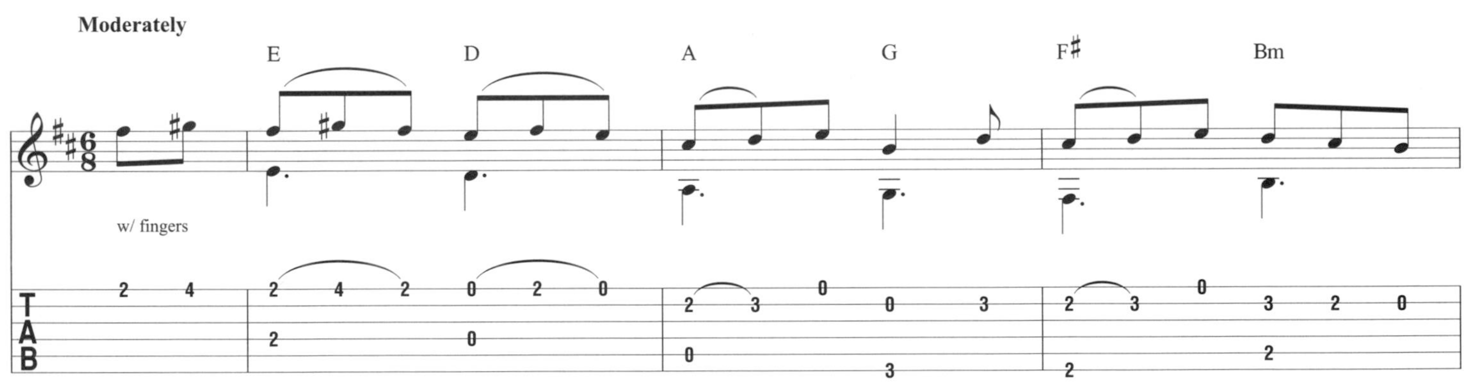

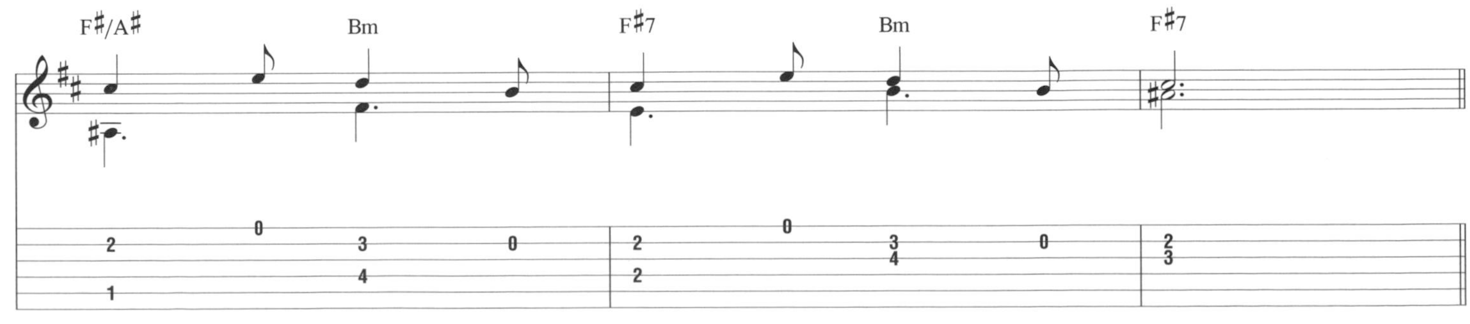

LICK 23

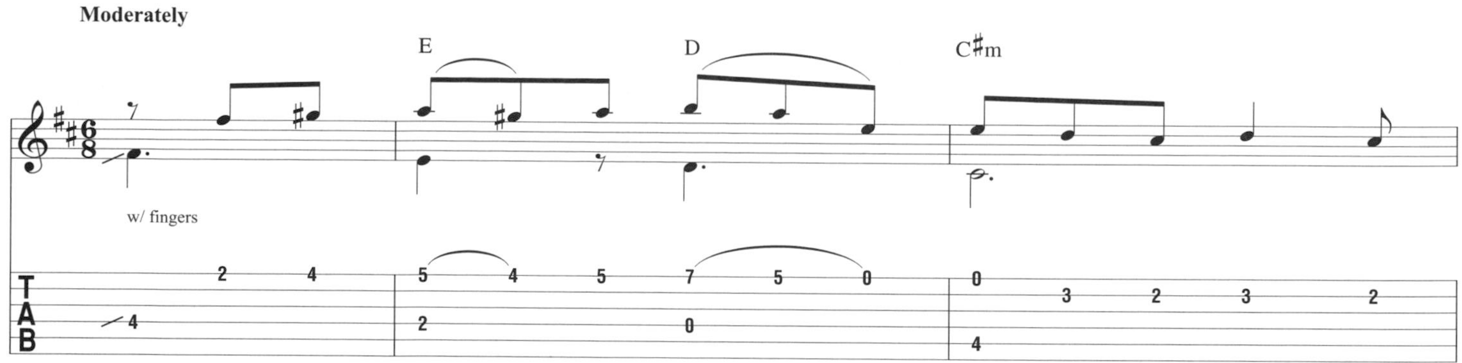

LICK 24

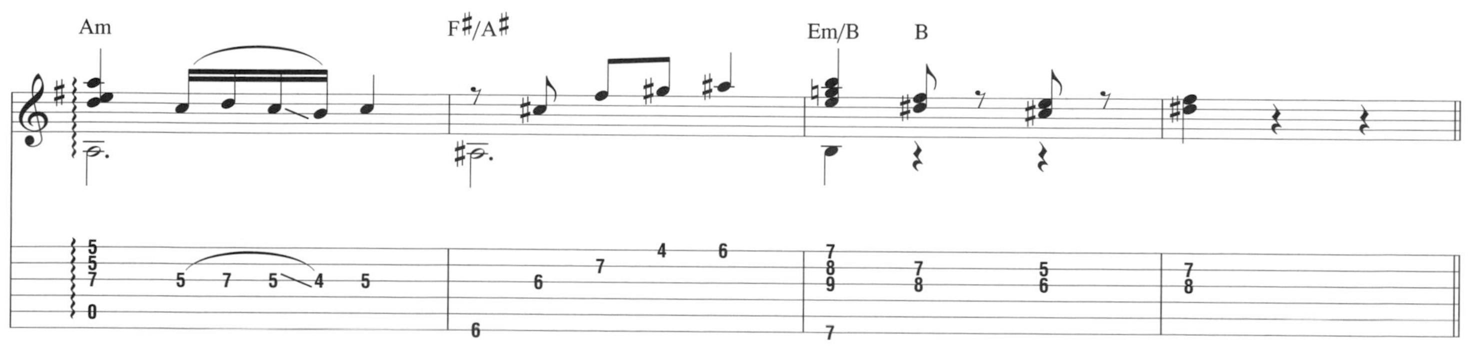

LICK 25

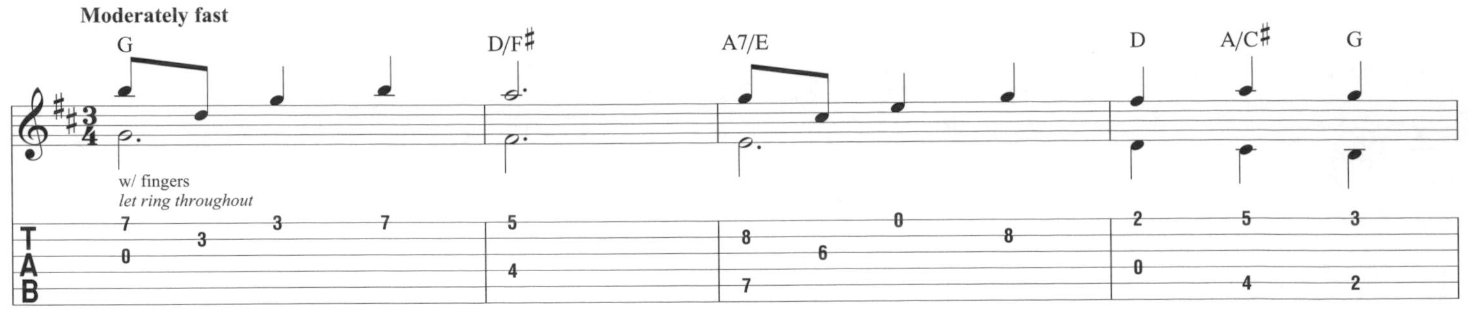

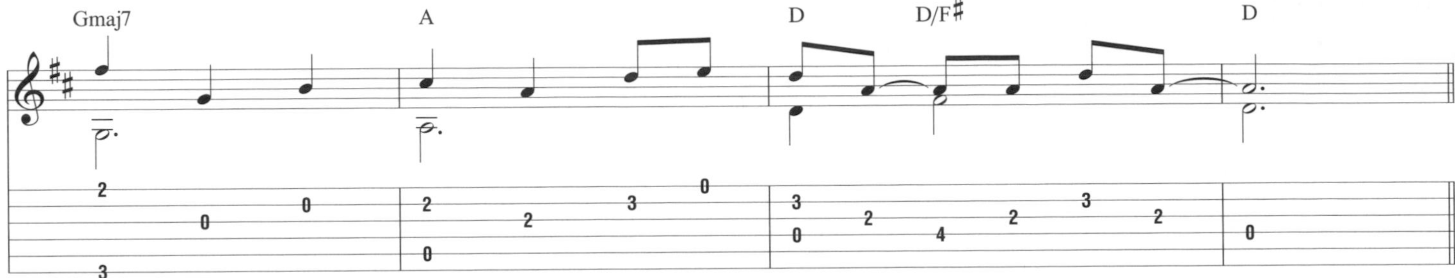

LICK 26

LICK 27

Blues

Blues evolved from plantation music and the work songs of black slaves who melded African pentatonic melody with European common-practice harmony. The acoustic guitar branch of the blues family tree was generally centered in the Mississippi Delta region of the American Deep South. It has a folk tradition and rose to prominence, largely through un-notated "oral tradition," in the years preceding World War II.

Acoustic blues guitar playing is generally epitomized by the traveling one-man band and is characteristically loose and improvisatory. The genre is exemplified by the varied acoustic styles of Leadbelly, Mississippi John Hurt, Robert Johnson, Charlie Patton, Skip James, Fred McDowell, Tommy Johnson, Lightnin' Hopkins, John Lee Hooker, Bukka White, Big Bill Broonzy, and Son House, among many others.

Acoustic blues and modern rock are inextricably linked through the work of players like Eric Clapton, Jimmy Page, Jimi Hendrix, and John Mayall. Many of these musicians adapted acoustic styles to their largely electric repertory or openly emulated the songs of their forebears in original form. Subsequently, acoustic blues has cropped up in the music of diverse '70s/'80s rock guitarists such as Richie Sambora (Bon Jovi's "Wanted Dead or Alive"), Steve Howe, Rik Emmett (Triumph's "Cool Down"), and Edward Van Halen ("Take Your Whiskey Home"). Acoustic blues enjoyed a revival in the '90s with the inception of MTV's *Unplugged* series and, more specifically, the appearances of Stevie Ray Vaughan and Eric Clapton.

Acoustic blues guitarists have historically adapted a variety of instruments to their needs. The standard steel-string acoustic was employed by Robert Johnson, Big Bill Broonzy, Scrapper Blackwell, Skip James, Fred McDowell, Lightnin' Hopkins, and John Lee Hooker. The acoustic resonator guitar is associated with Son House, Tampa Red, and Bukka White, while Bo Carter preferred a nylon-string instrument. Leadbelly used a 12-string acoustic, while Big Joe Williams played an atypical nine-string guitar. During the mid-'90s, the Martin guitar company issued two Eric Clapton models (000-28EC and 000-42EC) in response to his *Unplugged* success and the growing interest in Slowhand's acoustic blues styles.

LICK 28

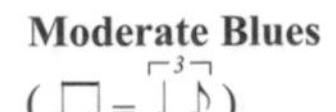
LICK 29

Moderate Blues
E7#9
w/ fingers
P.M. on ⑥
T
A
B

A7
E
P.M.
P.M. on ⑤

LICK 30

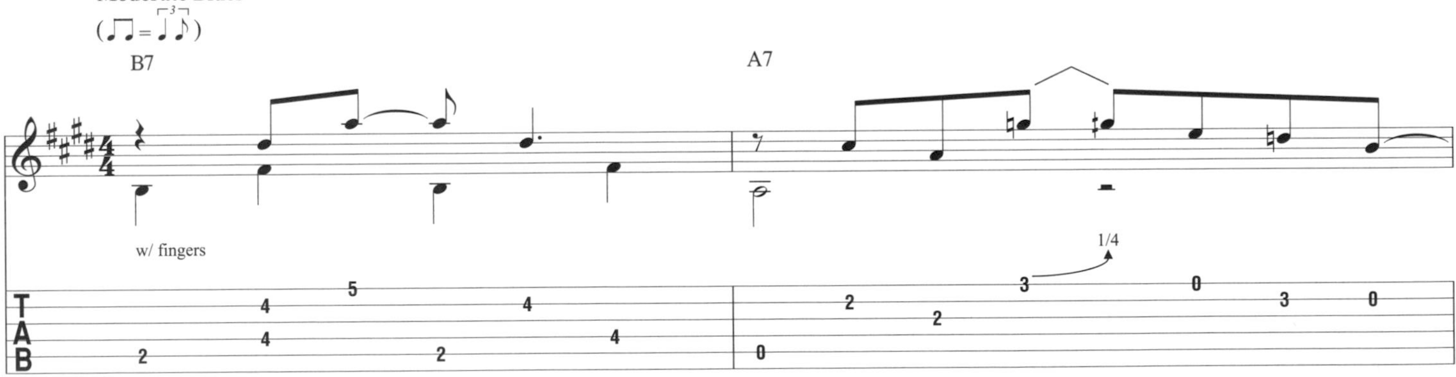
Moderate Blues
B7
A7
w/ fingers
1/4
T
A
B

E7

LICK 31

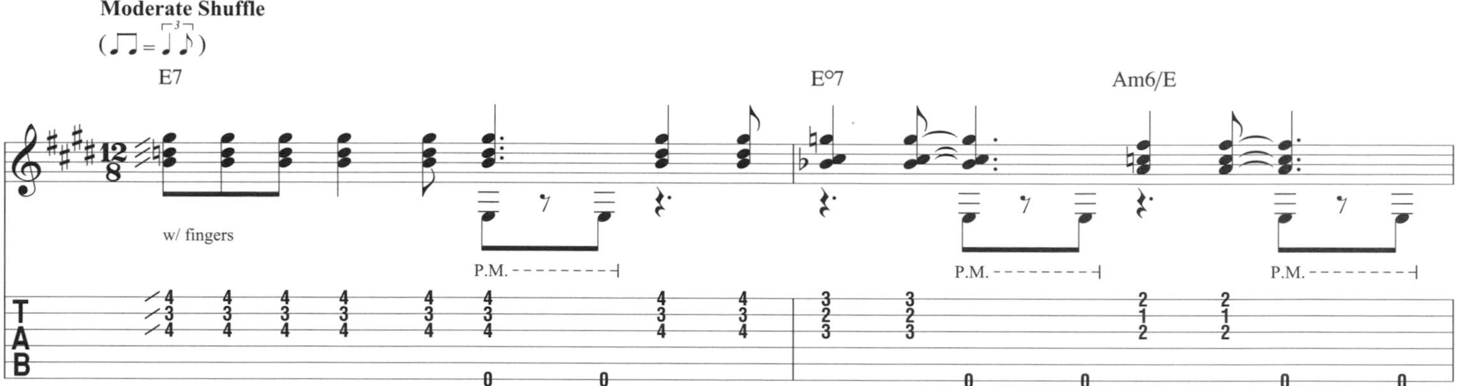

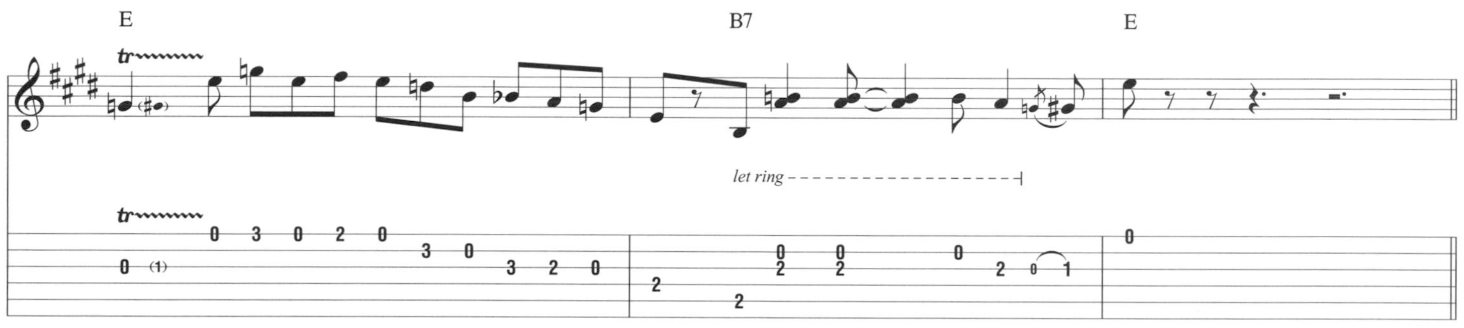

LICK 32

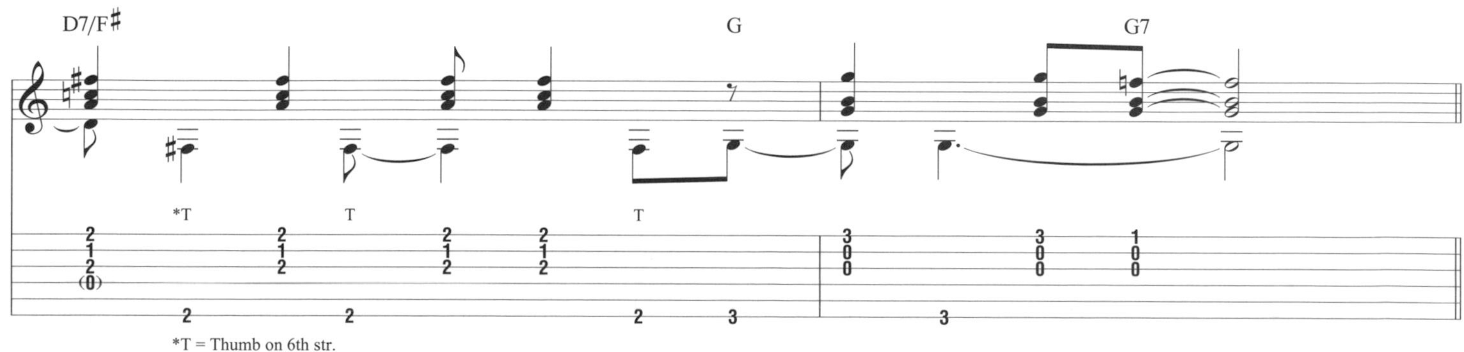

LICK 33

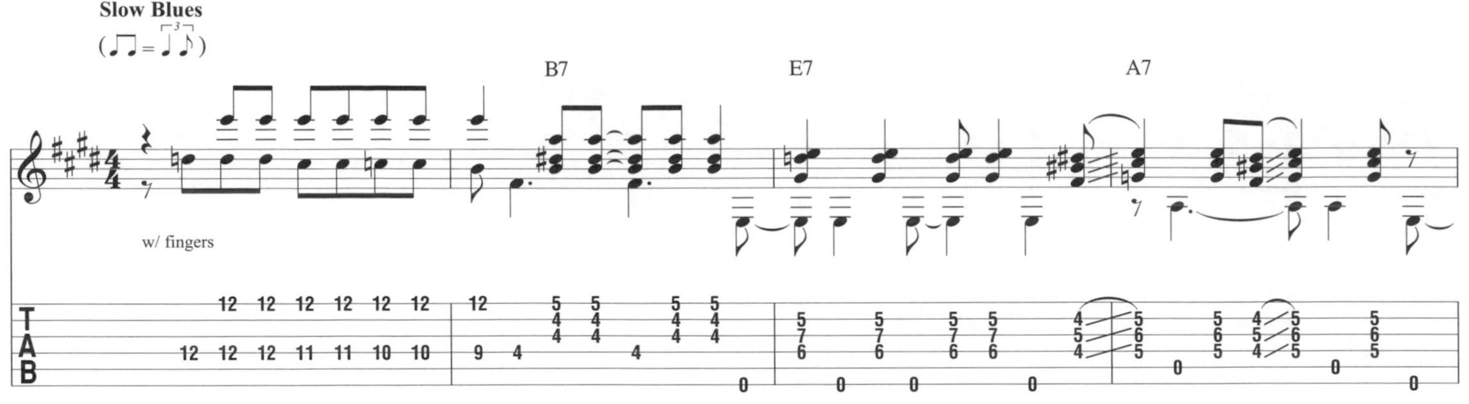

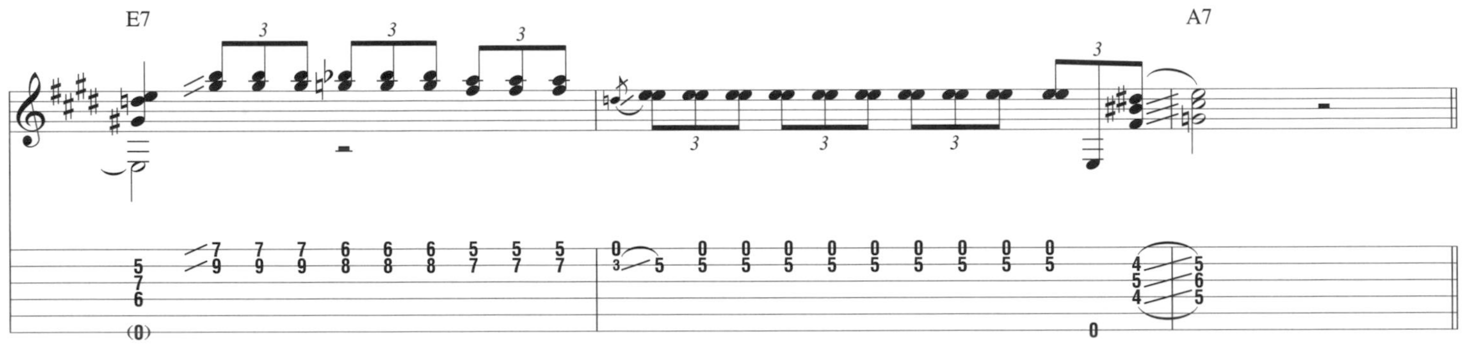

LICK 34

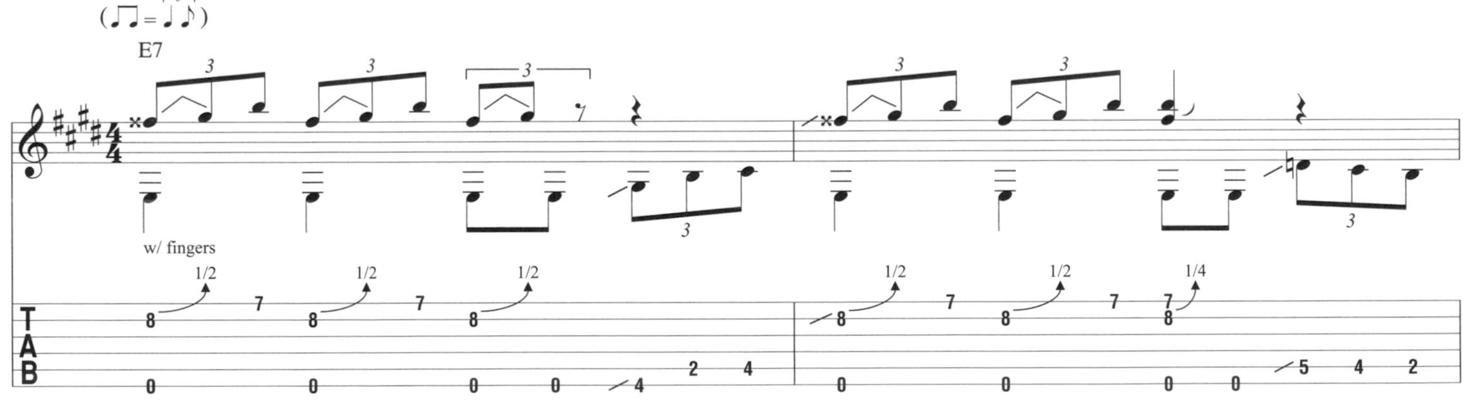

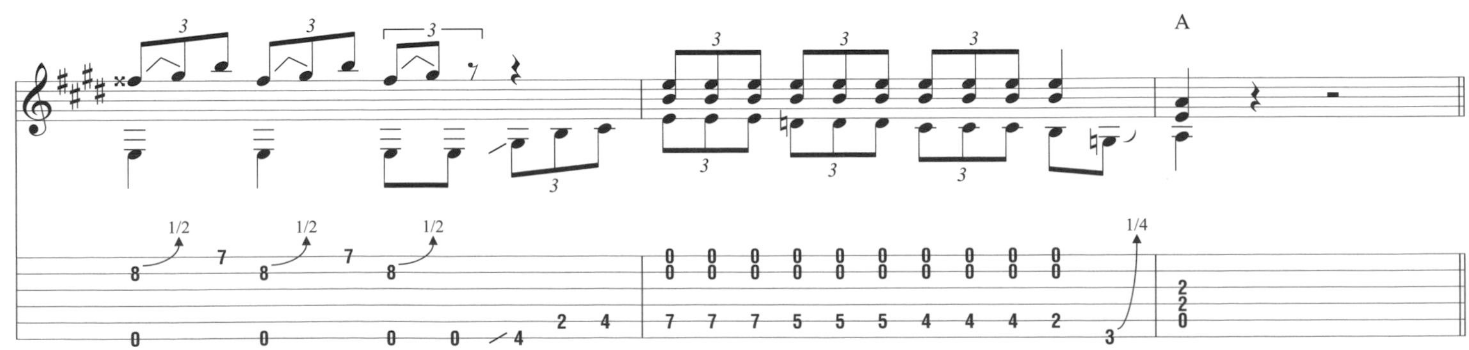

LICK 35

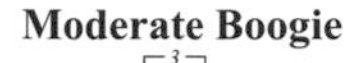
Moderate Boogie

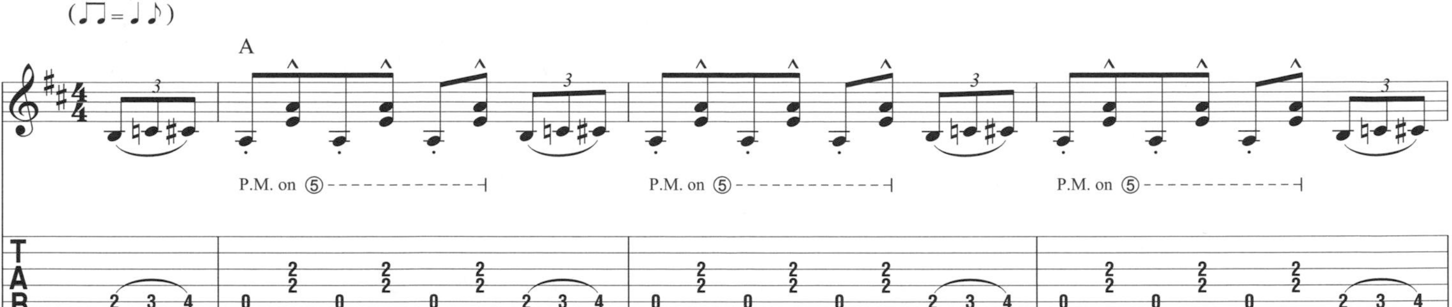
A
3
P.M. on ⑤
T
A
B
2 3 4
0 2 2 0 2 2 0 2 2 2 3 4

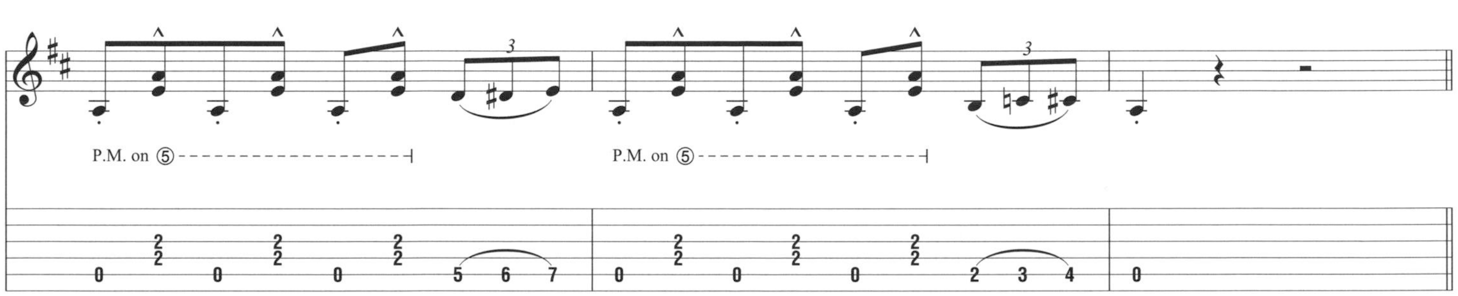
3
P.M. on ⑤
0 2 2 0 2 2 0 2 2 5 6 7
0 2 2 0 2 2 0 2 2 2 3 4
0

Pop and Rock

The acoustic guitar has been part of popular music since the '20s, when acoustic rhythm and lead players like Eddie Lang backed singers such as Bing Crosby on the earliest recordings and radio performances. As pop music grew into an industry, whether produced in Hollywood, New York, or Nashville, acoustic guitar colors figured prominently in studio-crafted arrangements dominating the hit parade.

When rock 'n' roll entered the world's pop consciousness in the '50s, it became a driving force in music. As a result, the acoustic guitar was seen and heard regularly in the music of Elvis Presley, Rick Nelson, the Everly Brothers, Gene Vincent, Johnny Cash, and Roy Orbison. The folk explosion and its popular success in the early '60s, personified by Bob Dylan, the Kingston Trio, Peter, Paul & Mary, Joan Baez, et al., merged the traditions of Appalachia, English folk music, bluegrass, and simple country story songs.

A few years later, the Beatles established a lasting legacy of acoustic pop/rock guitar work during the British Invasion. The trend continued into the ensuing decades with singer-songwriters Paul Simon, James Taylor, Cat Stevens, Jim Croce, Joni Mitchell, and countless others. And practically every major artist, regardless of genre, appeared in acoustic trappings to hawk their acoustic wares and participate in the *Unplugged* movement of the '90s. That tradition still resounds in rock and pop, reflected in the output of Melissa Etheridge, John Mayer, Dave Matthews, and Sheryl Crow.

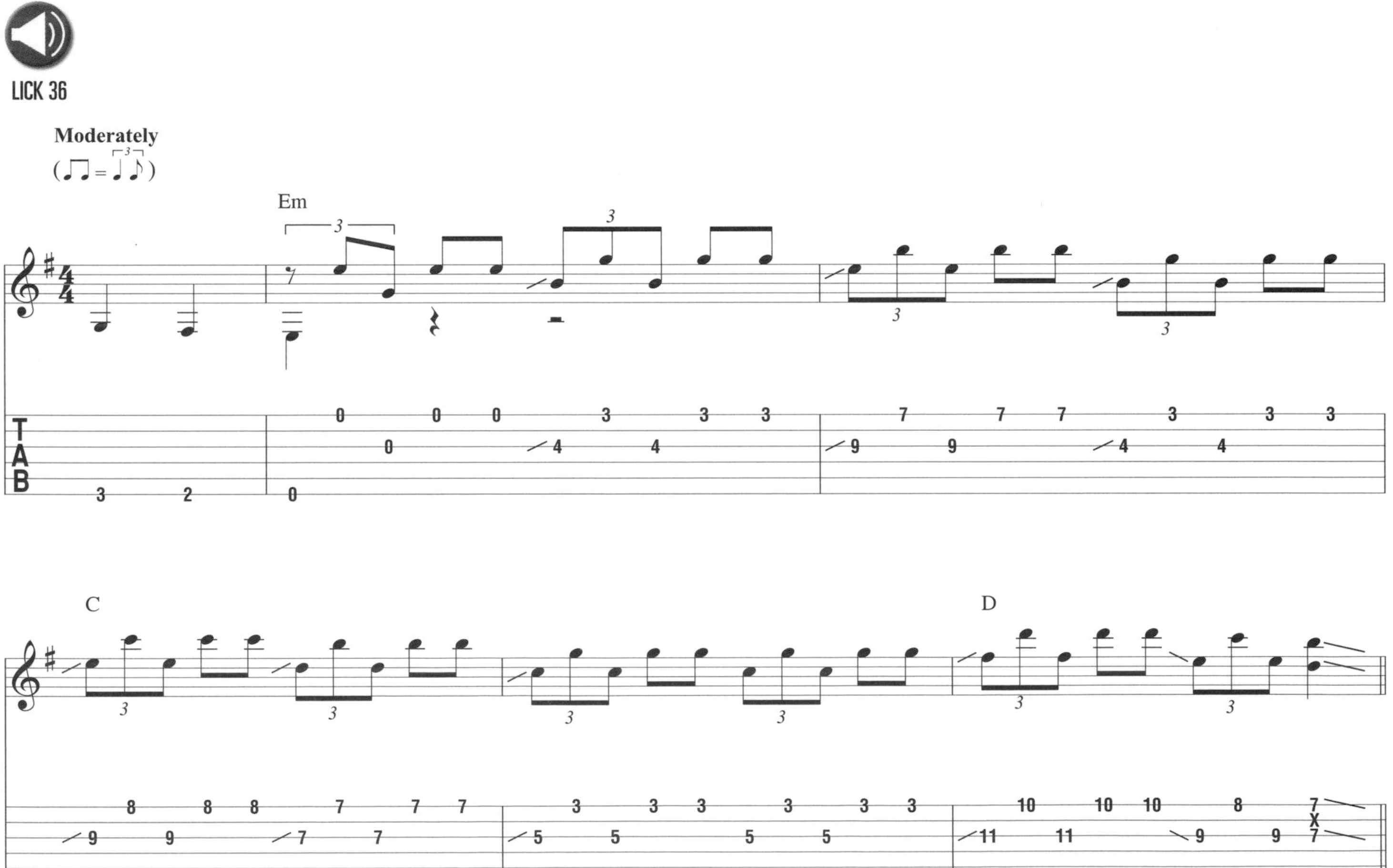

LICK 37

LICK 38

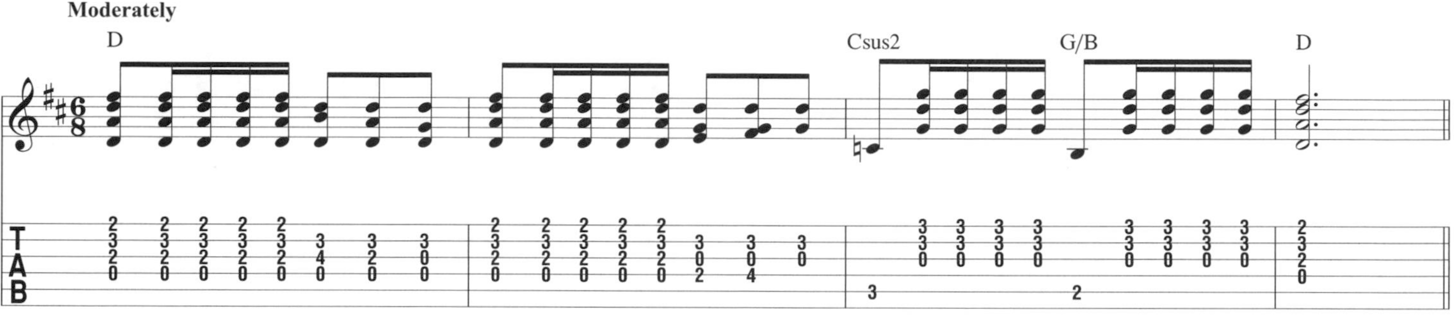

LICK 39

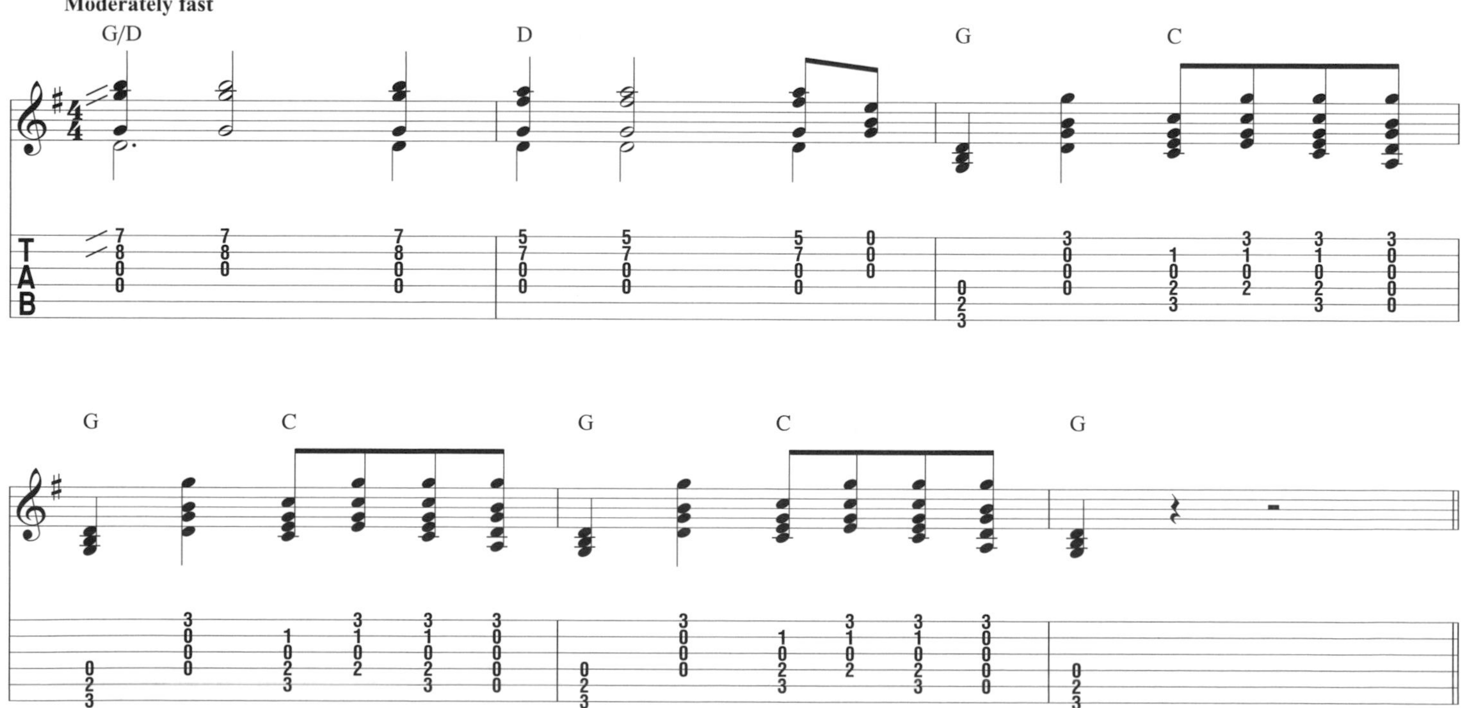

LICK 40

LICK 41

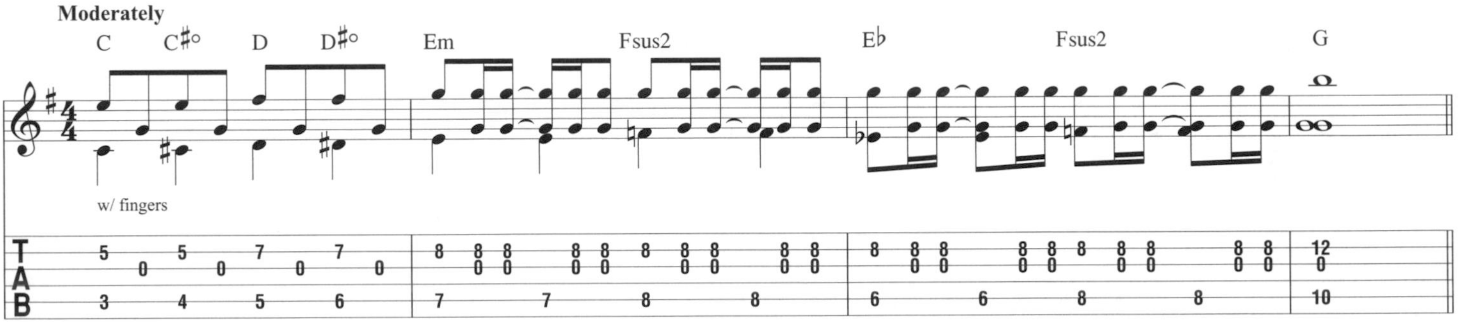

LICK 42

LICK 43

LICK 44

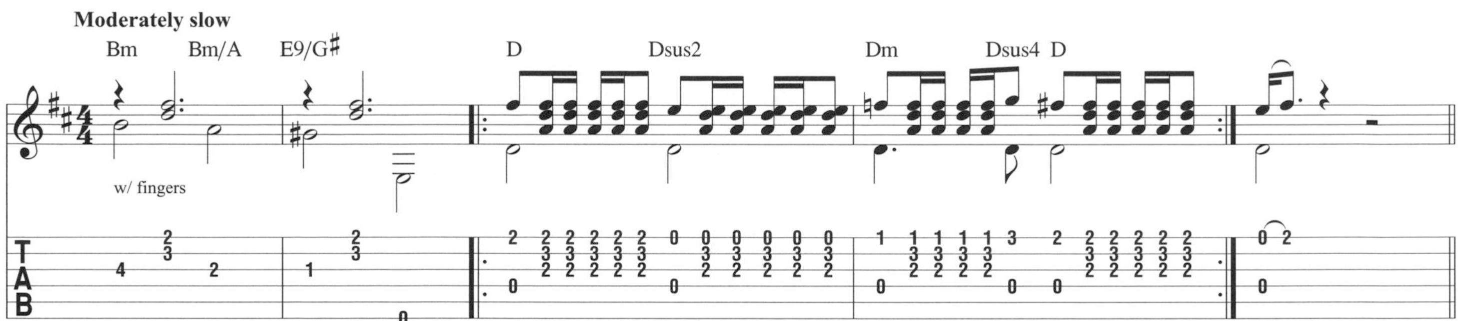

LICK 45

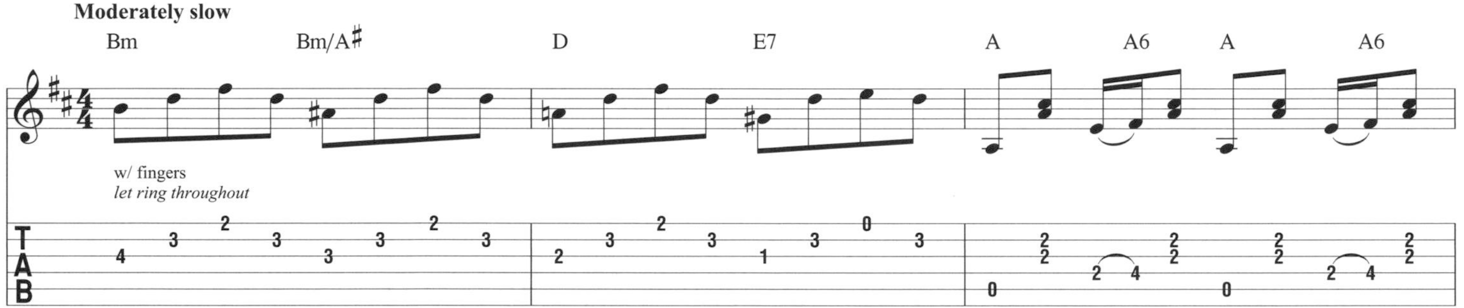

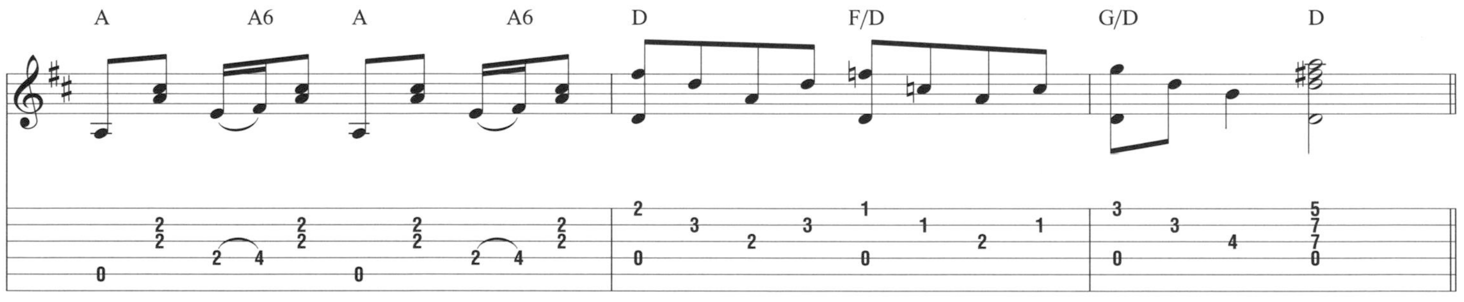

LICK 46

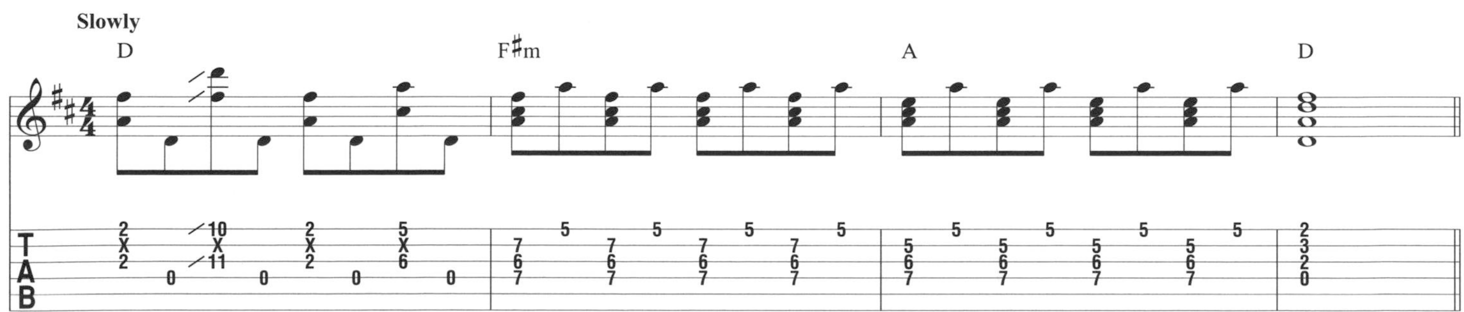

LICK 47

Capo VII

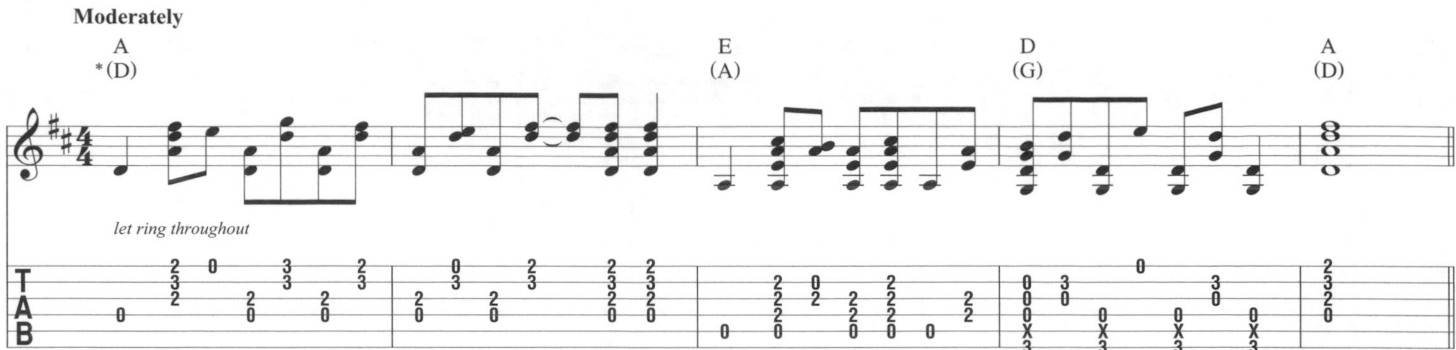

*Symbols in parentheses represent chord names respective to capoed guitar.
Symbols above reflect actual sounding chords. Capoed fret is "0" in tab.

LICK 48

Capo VII

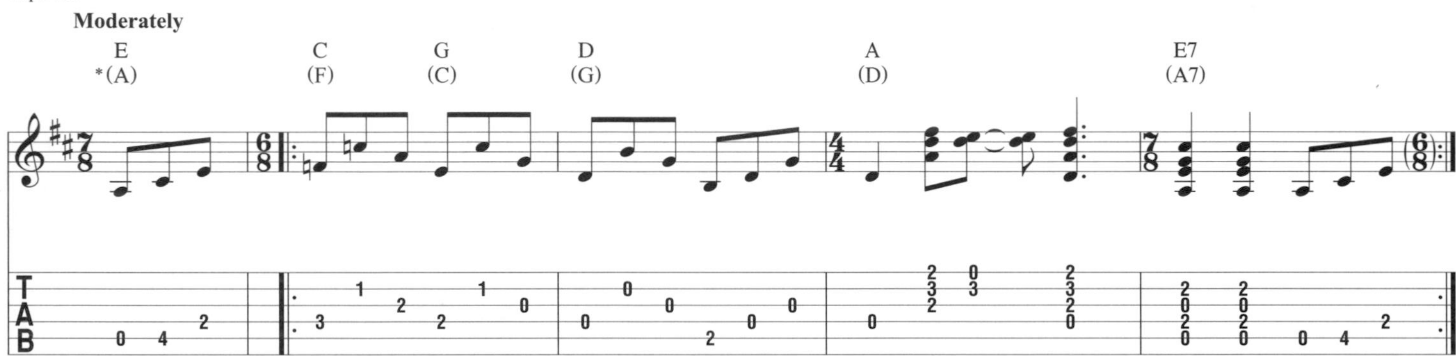

*Symbols in parentheses represent chord names respective to capoed guitar.
Symbols above reflect actual sounding chords. Capoed fret is "0" in tab.

LICK 49

Capo V

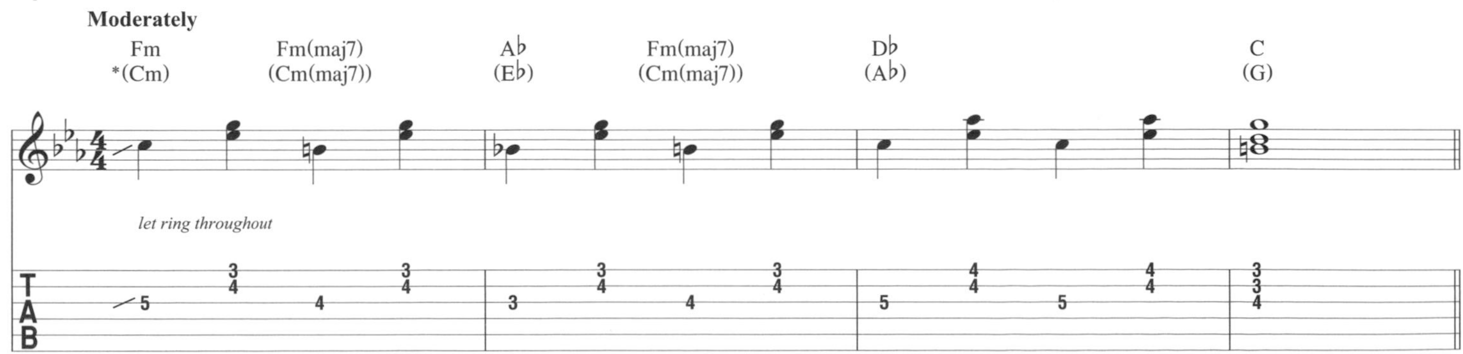

*Symbols in parentheses represent chord names respective to capoed guitar.
Symbols above reflect actual sounding chords. Capoed fret is "0" in tab.

LICK 50

Moderately slow Shuffle

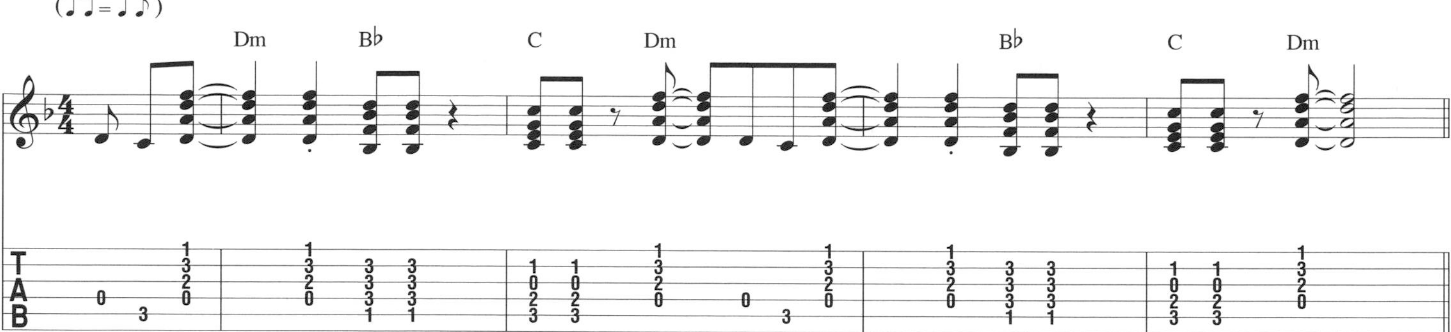

LICK 51

Moderately

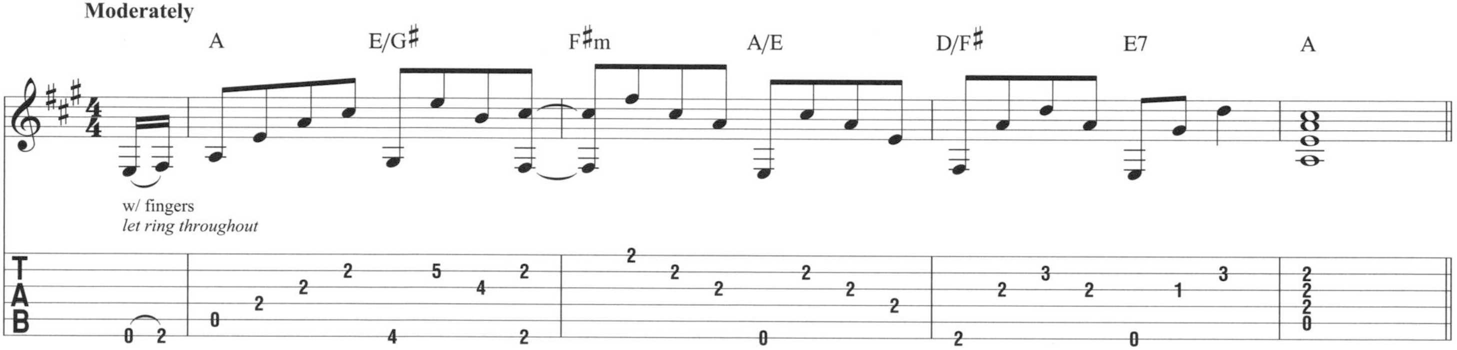

LICK 52

Moderately

LICK 53

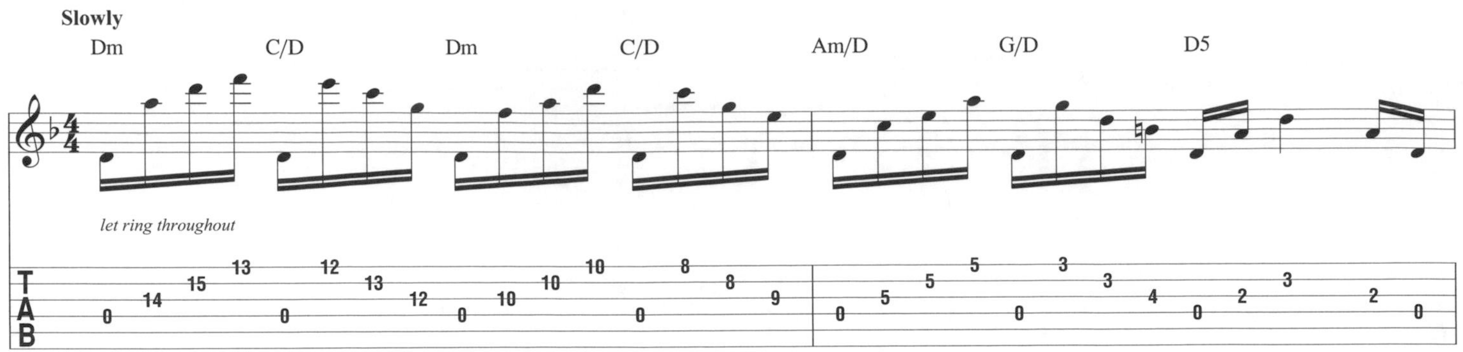

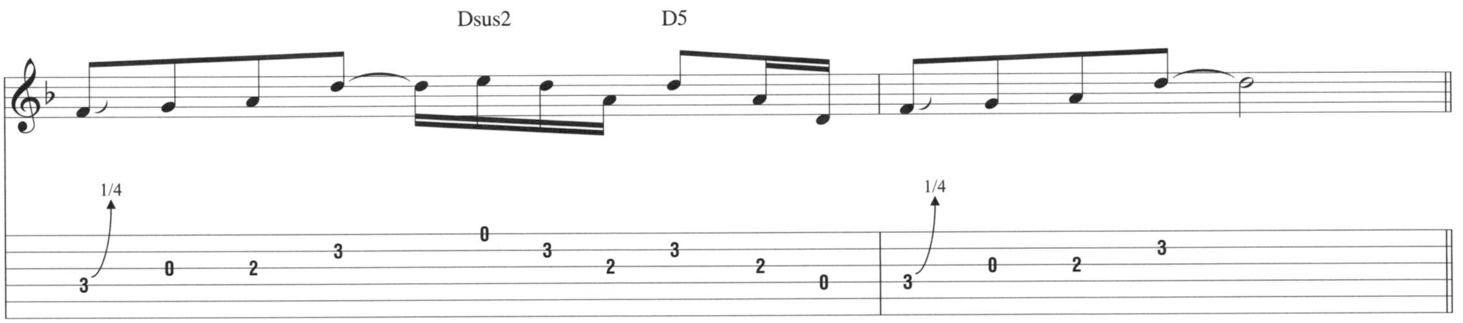

LICK 54

LICK 55

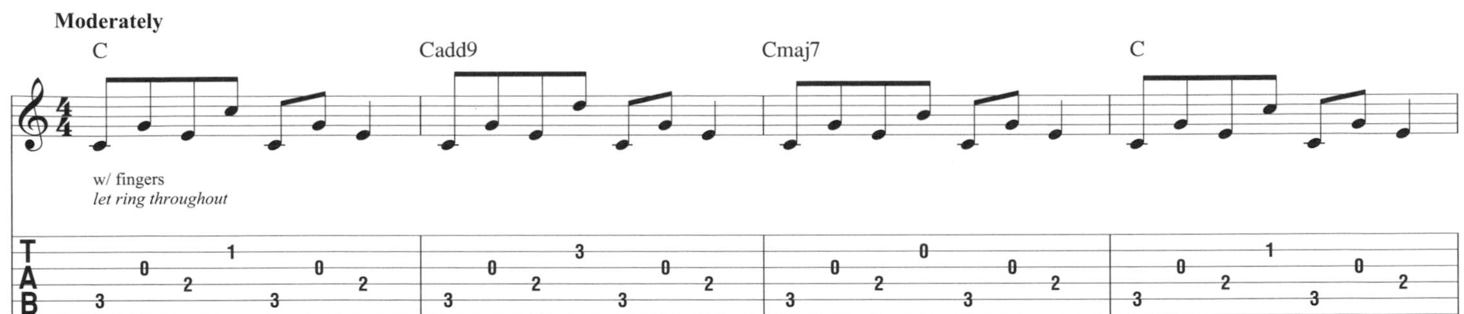
Moderately
C
Cadd9
Cmaj7
C
w/ fingers
let ring throughout
T
A
B

Am
Asus4
Asus2
Am
G/B
C

LICK 56

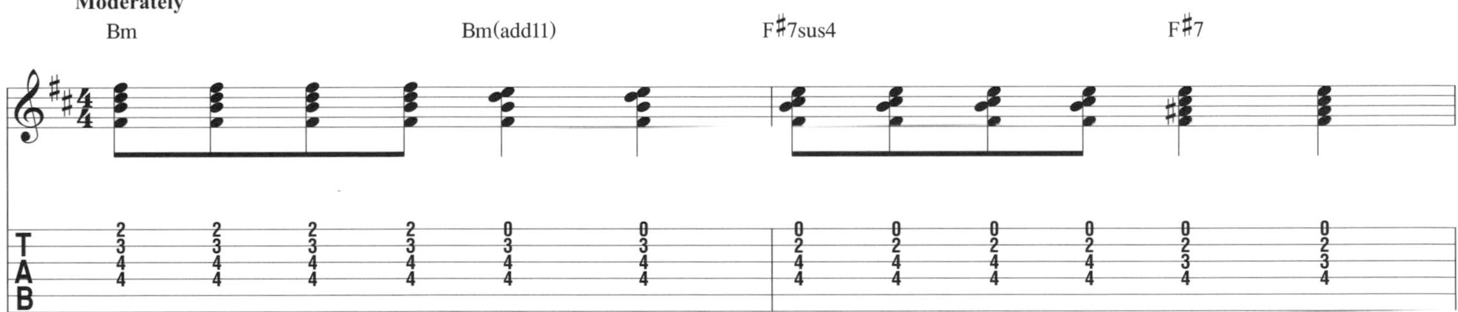
Moderately
Bm
Bm(add11)
F♯7sus4
F♯7
T
A
B

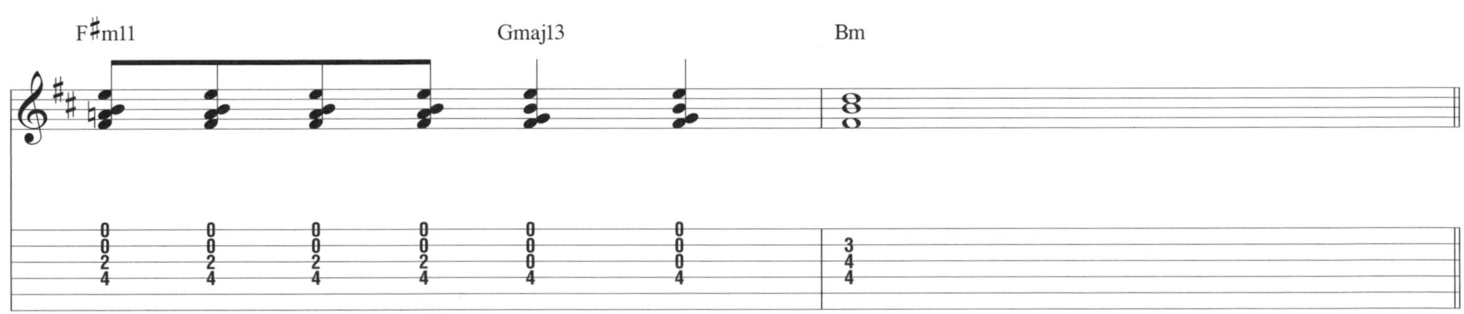
F♯m11
Gmaj13
Bm

LICK 57

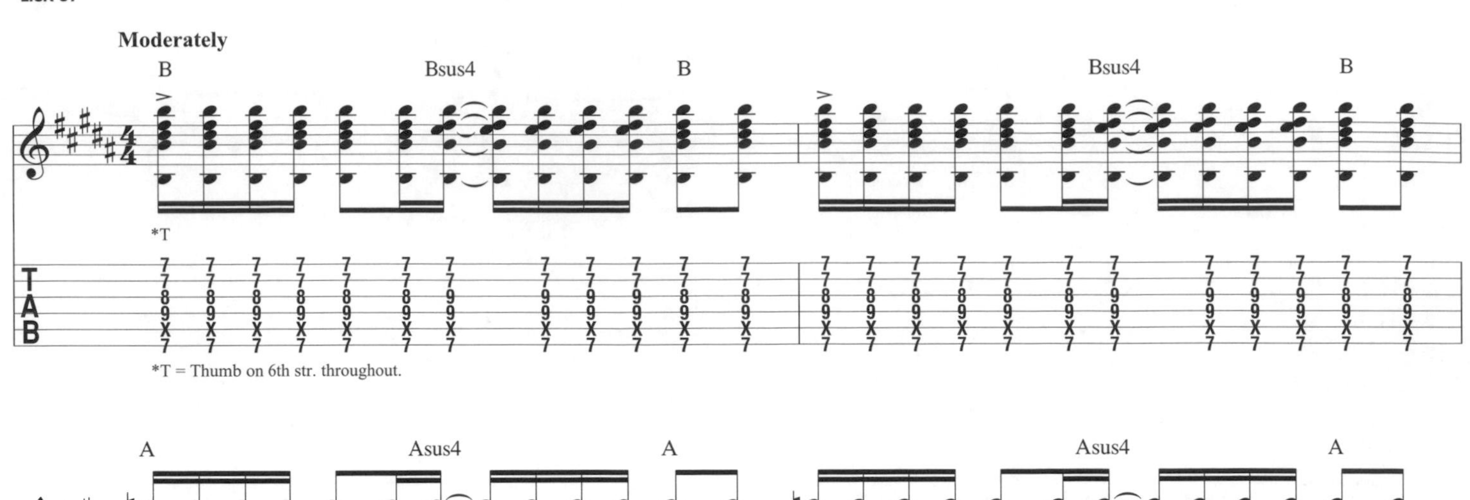

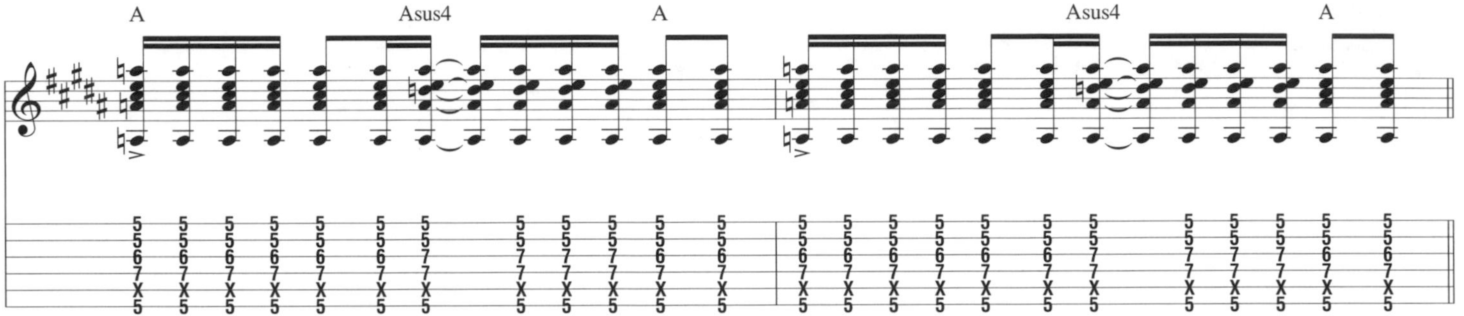

LICK 58

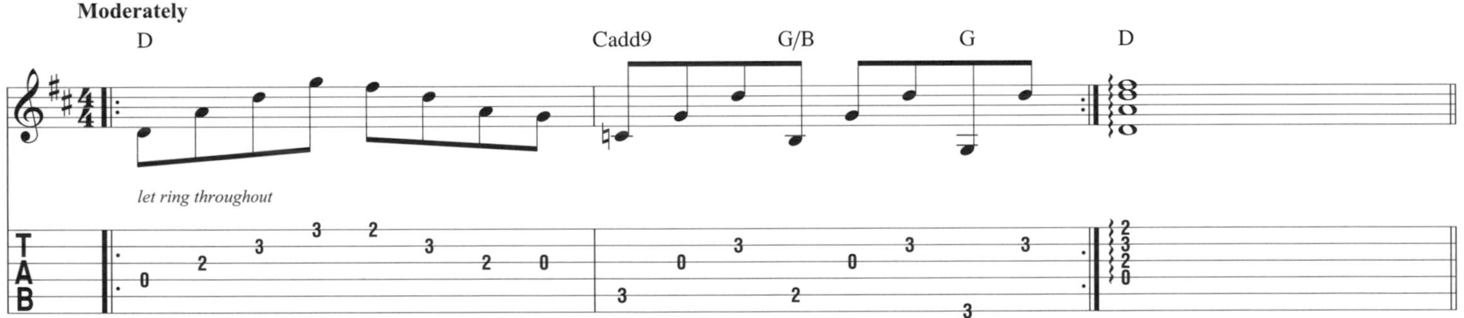

LICK 59

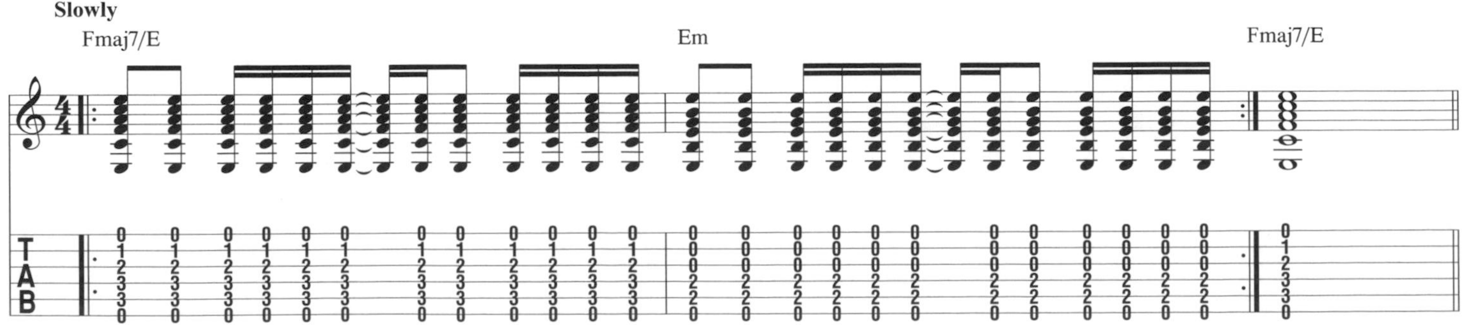

LICK 60

Capo III

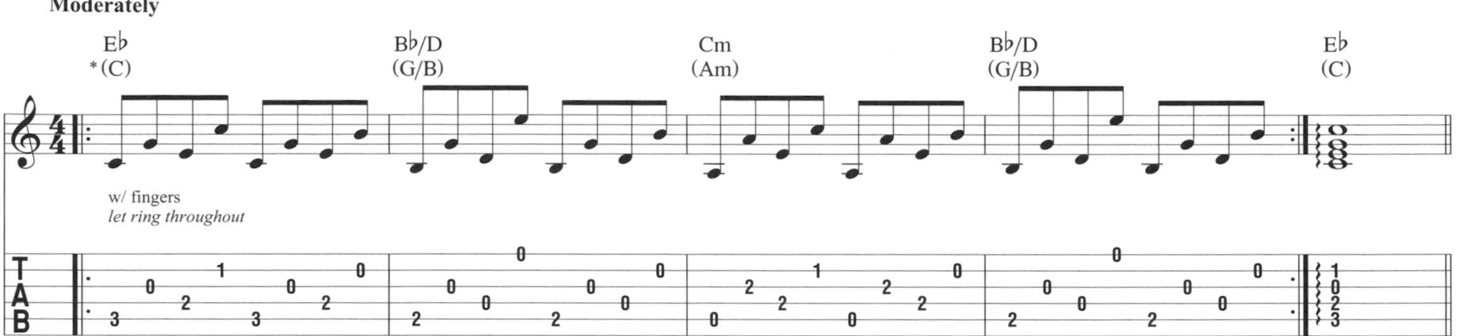

*Symbols in parentheses represent chord names respective to capoed guitar. Symbols above reflect actual sounding chords. Capoed fret is "0" in tab.

LICK 61

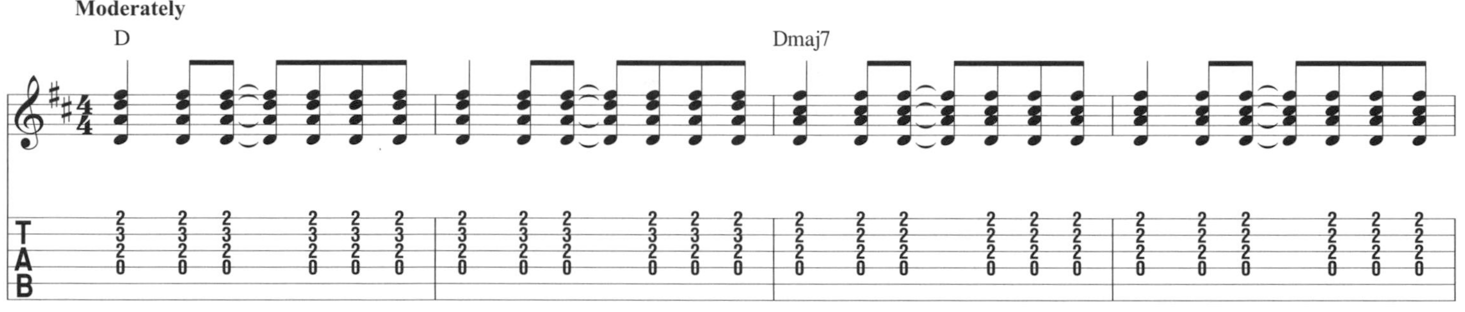

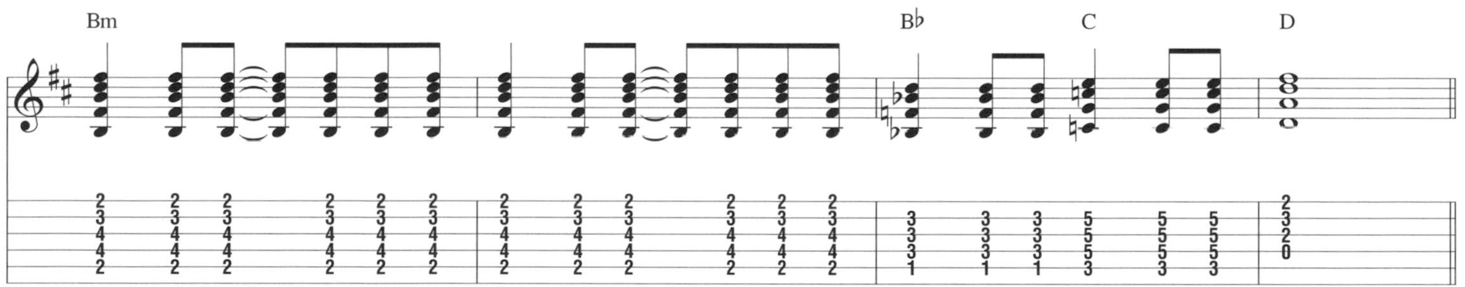

LICK 62

Drop D tuning:
(low to high) D–A–D–G–B–E

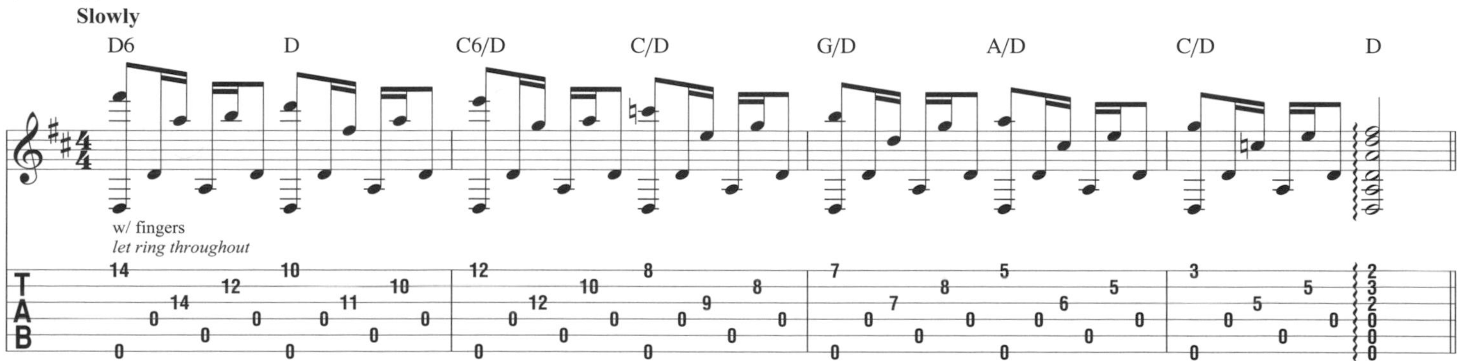

LICK 63

Drop D tuning:
(low to high) D–A–D–G–B–E

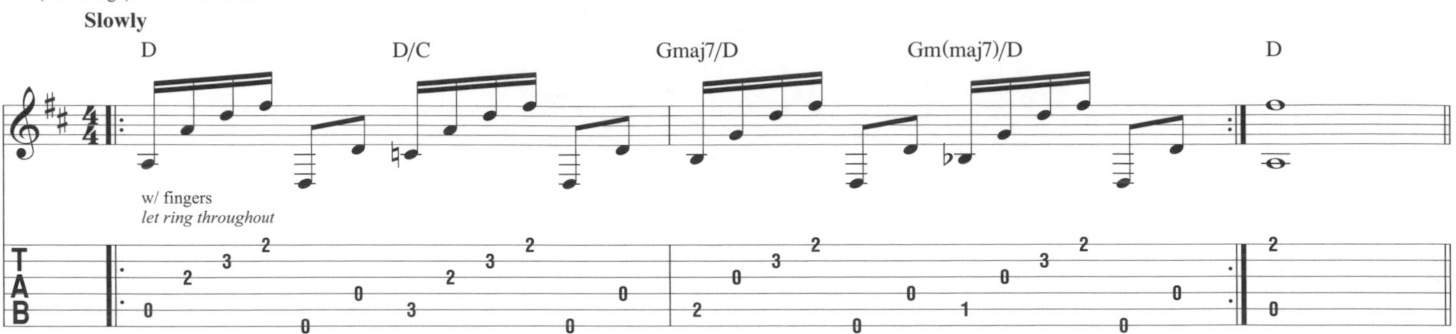

LICK 64

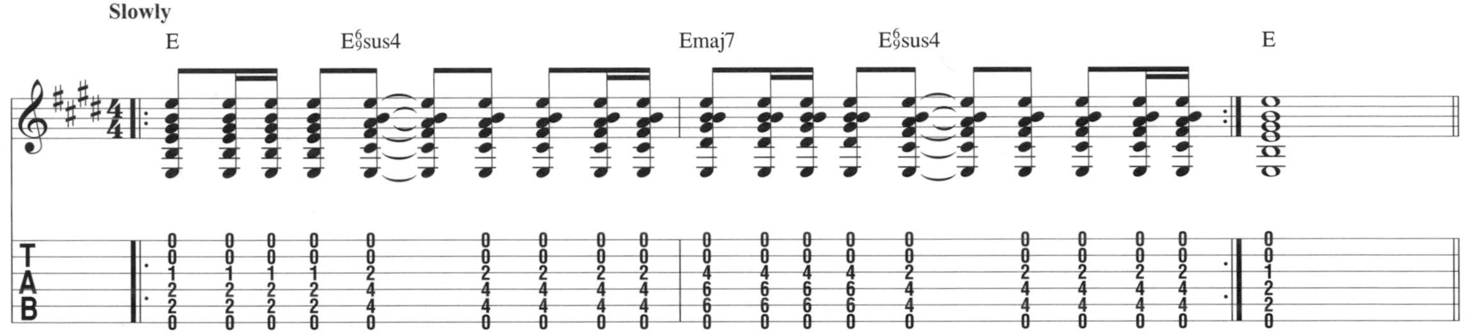

LICK 65

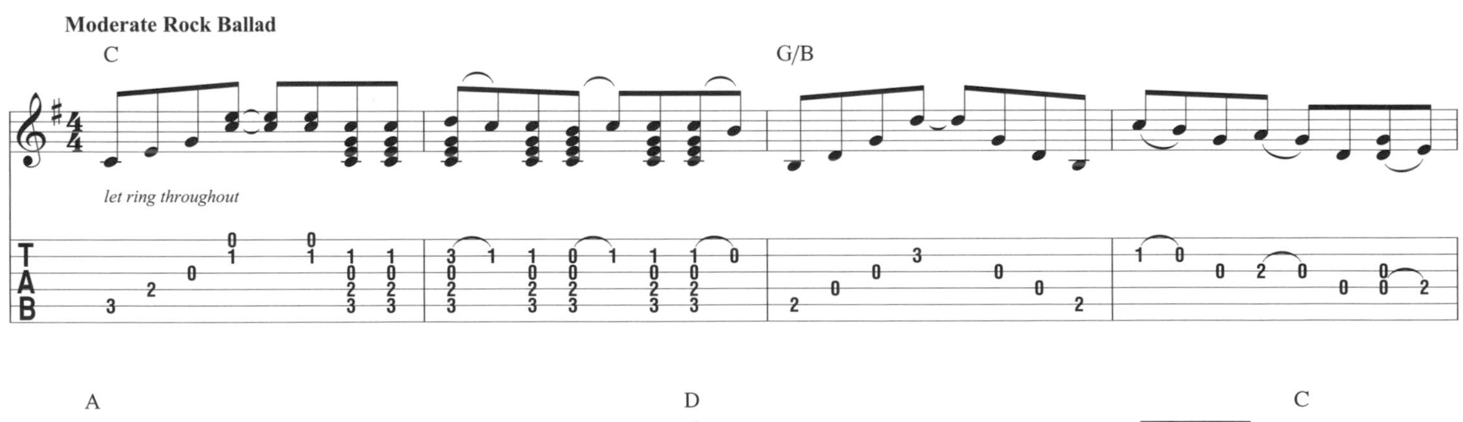

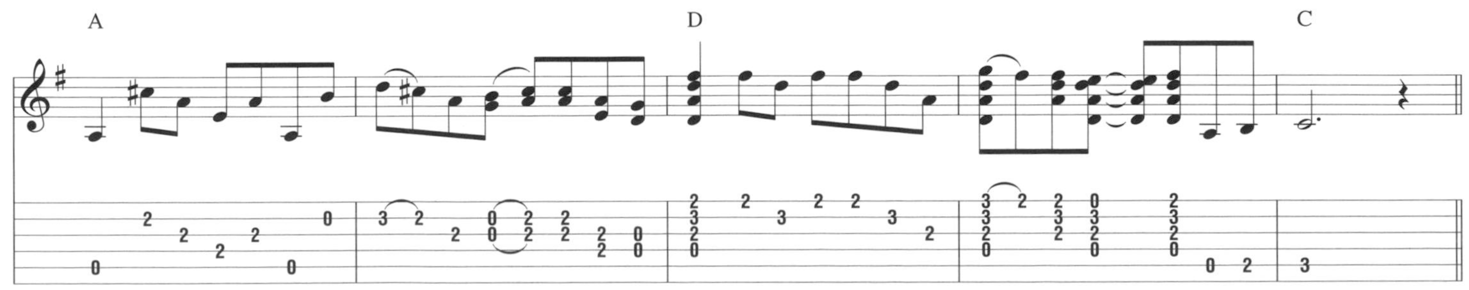

LICK 66

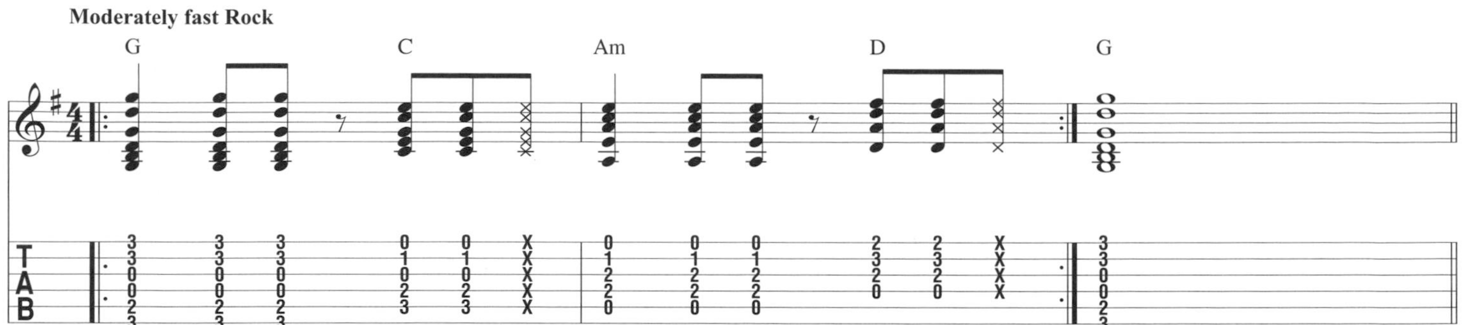

LICK 67

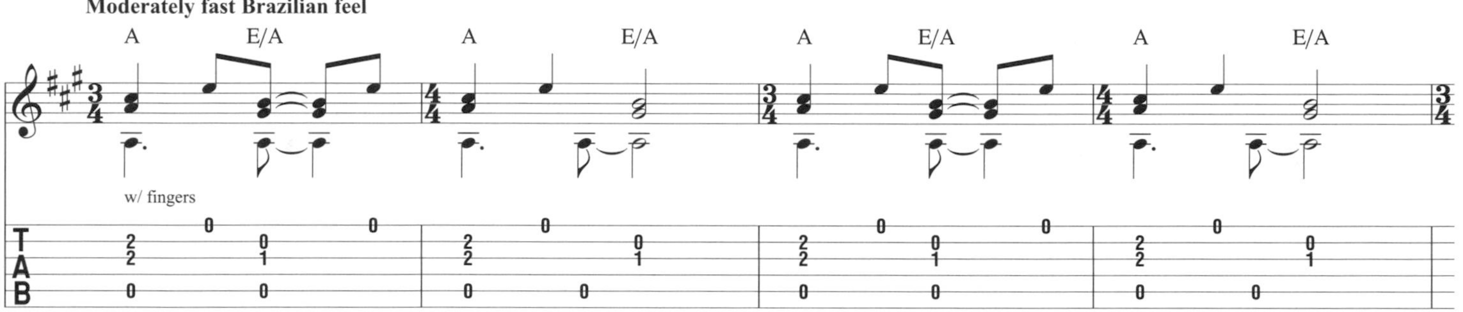

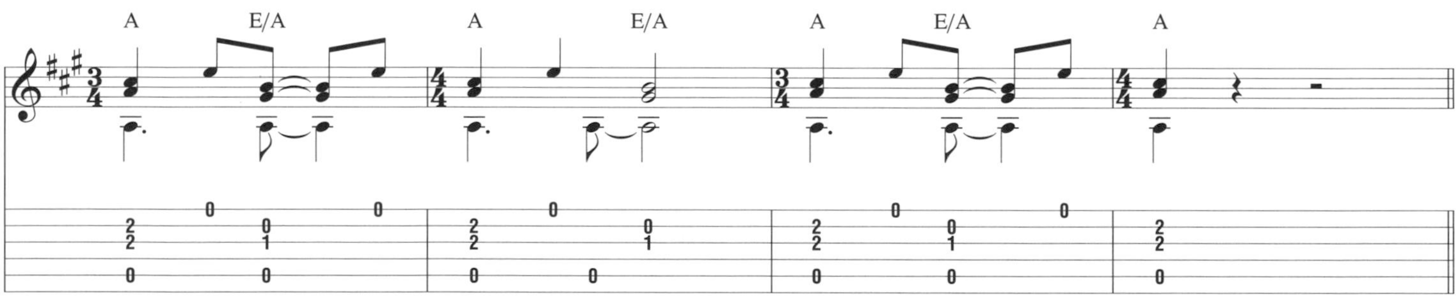

LICK 68

*Nashville tuning:
(low to high): E↑–A↑–D↑–G↑–B–E

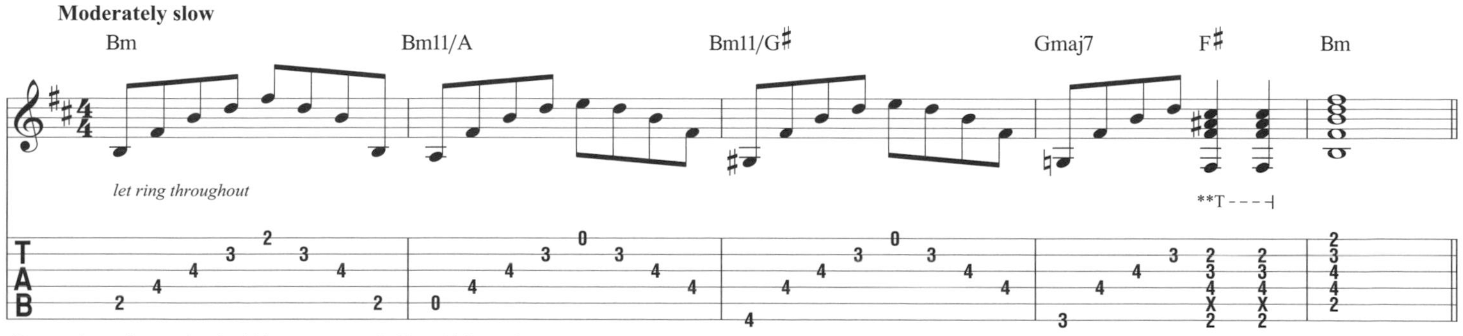

*Bottom four strings replaced w/ thinner gauges to facilitate higher tuning.
Notation refects normally tuned gtr. for ease of reading.

**T = Thumb on 6th str.

LICK 69

LICK 70

LICK 71

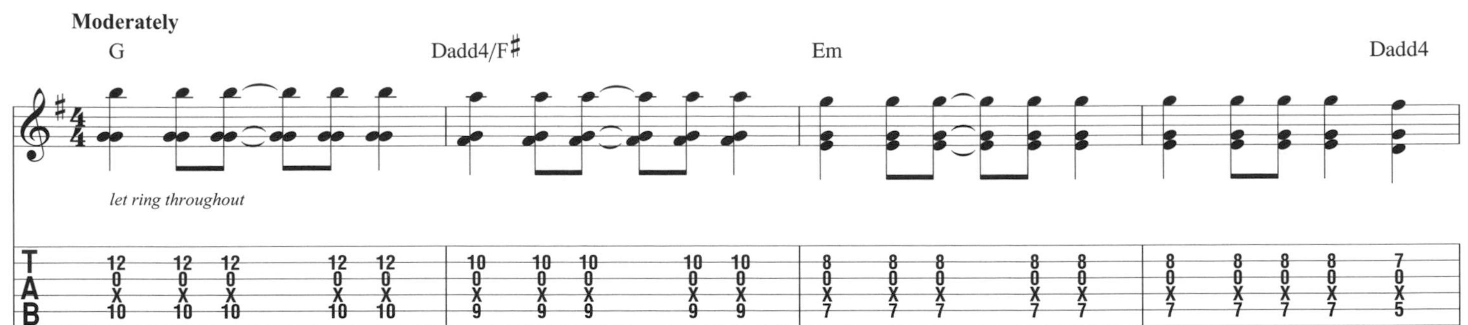

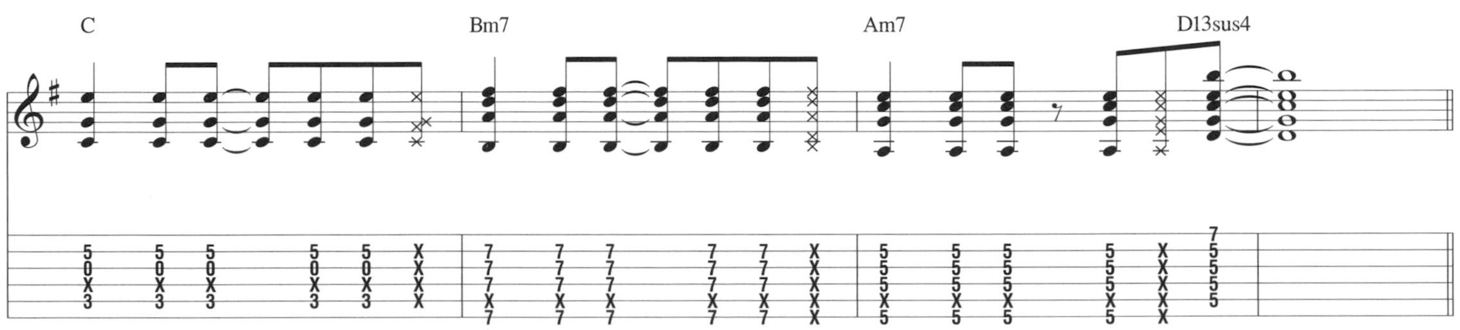

LICK 72

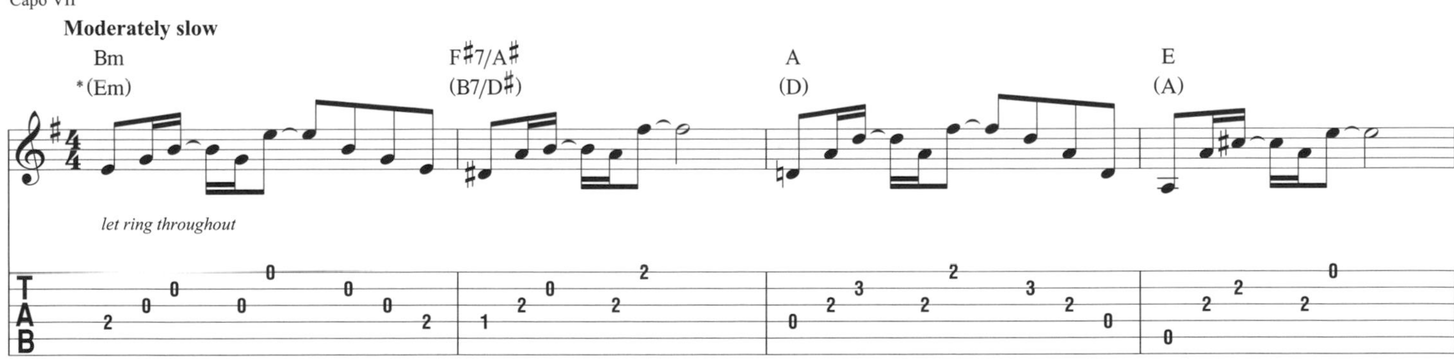

*Symbols in parentheses represent chord names respective to capoed guitar. Symbols above reflect actual sounding chords. Capoed fret is "0" in tab.

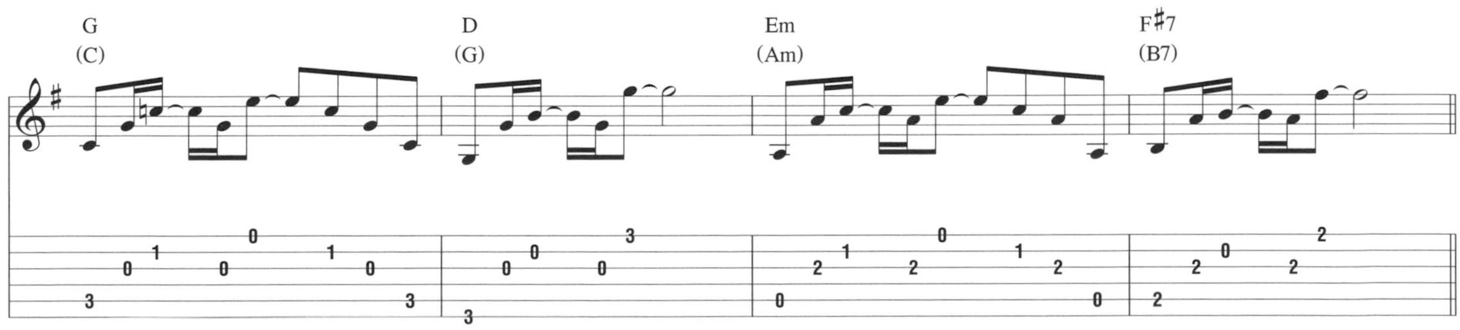

LICK 73

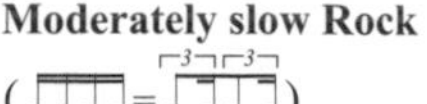

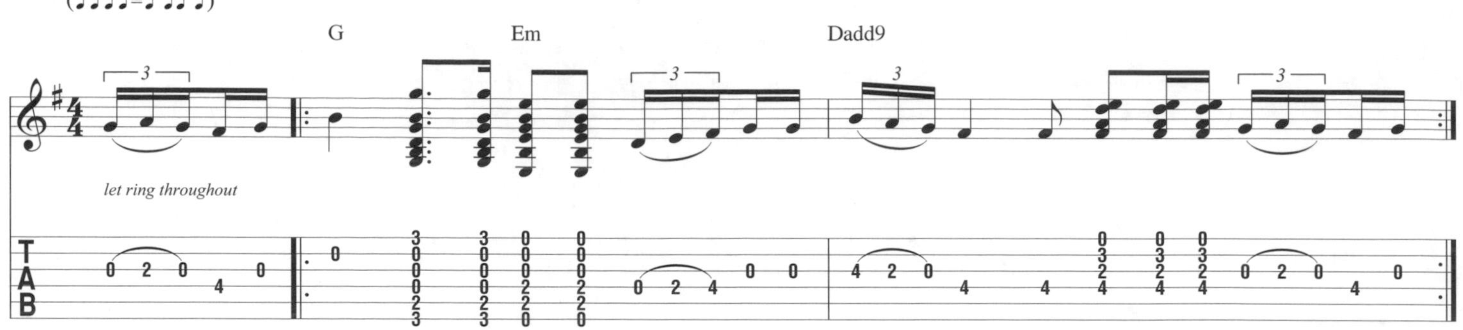

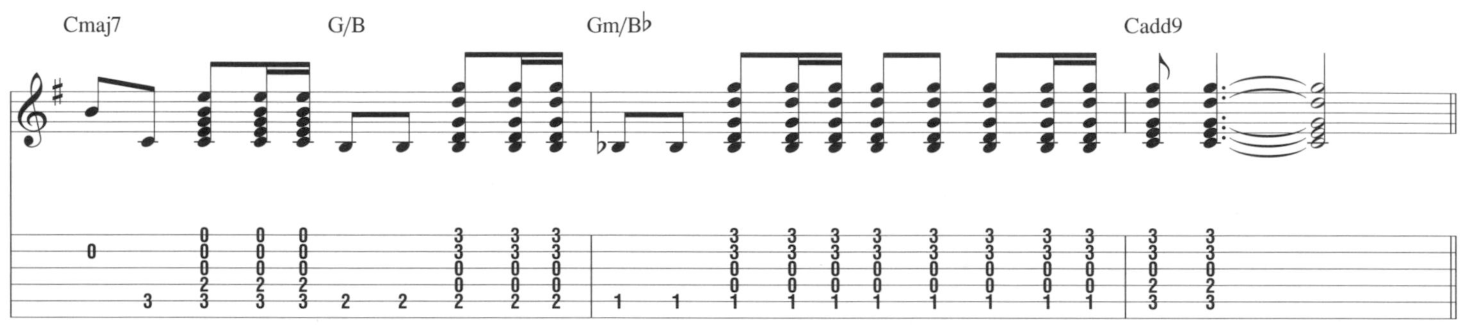

LICK 74

Moderately

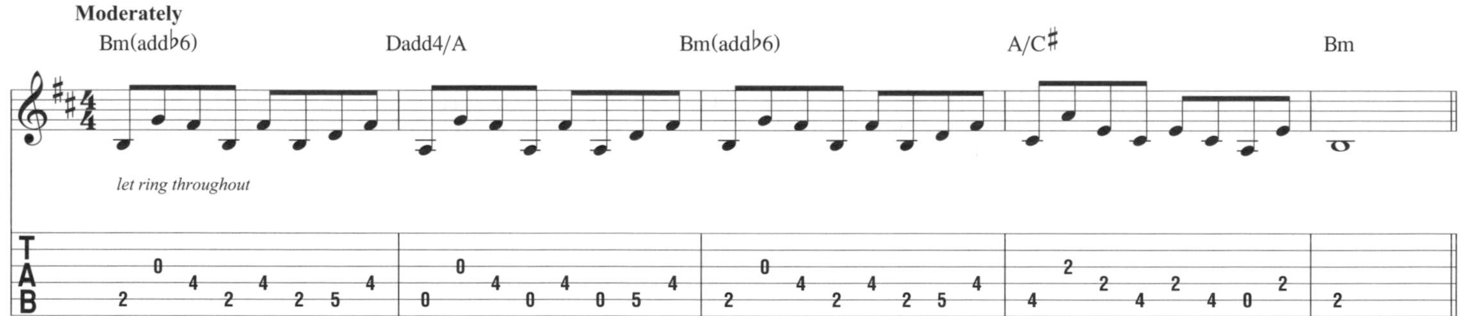

Folk and Folk Rock

The acoustic guitar and folk music have been virtually inseparable since time immemorial. The troubadours and trouvères of 12th-century Europe were the historic antecedents of artists like Bob Dylan, the Kingston Trio, and Peter, Paul & Mary. The Spartan texture of monophonic melody over a simple, slow-moving rhythmic/harmonic background on a string instrument (generally strummed or lightly arpeggiated) has remained a primary feature of folk music through the ages.

Technically, there are many forms of folk music in various cultures globally; however, the generally acknowledged "default" term, particularly as relates to the guitar tradition, refers to the American style. This form of folk music is the shorthand term for an evolving American style whose traditions grew out of Appalachian roots, transplanted Anglo folk songs of Scotland, Ireland, and Britain, and the narrative odes of the troubadours. Over the years, American folk music absorbed and was enriched by elements of bluegrass, country & western, Tex-Mex, Caribbean, rural blues, and jug band music, resulting in a multifarious mix of influences and tangents.

The reliance on and exploitation of modes in folk music is apparent; modal harmony is generally more conducive to the genre's simpler melody lines and narrower range. The influence of modal chord progressions and modal tunings—common in folk styles and often combined with the genre's simpler rhythmic motion and slower chord changes—can be heard variously in Jimmy Page's Zeppelin folk and Celtic acoustic work of "Tangerine," "That's the Way," and "Black Mountain Side," Steve Stills' dulcimer-like modality in "Suite: Judy Blue Eyes," and Duane Allman's country/folk/blues amalgam in "Little Martha."

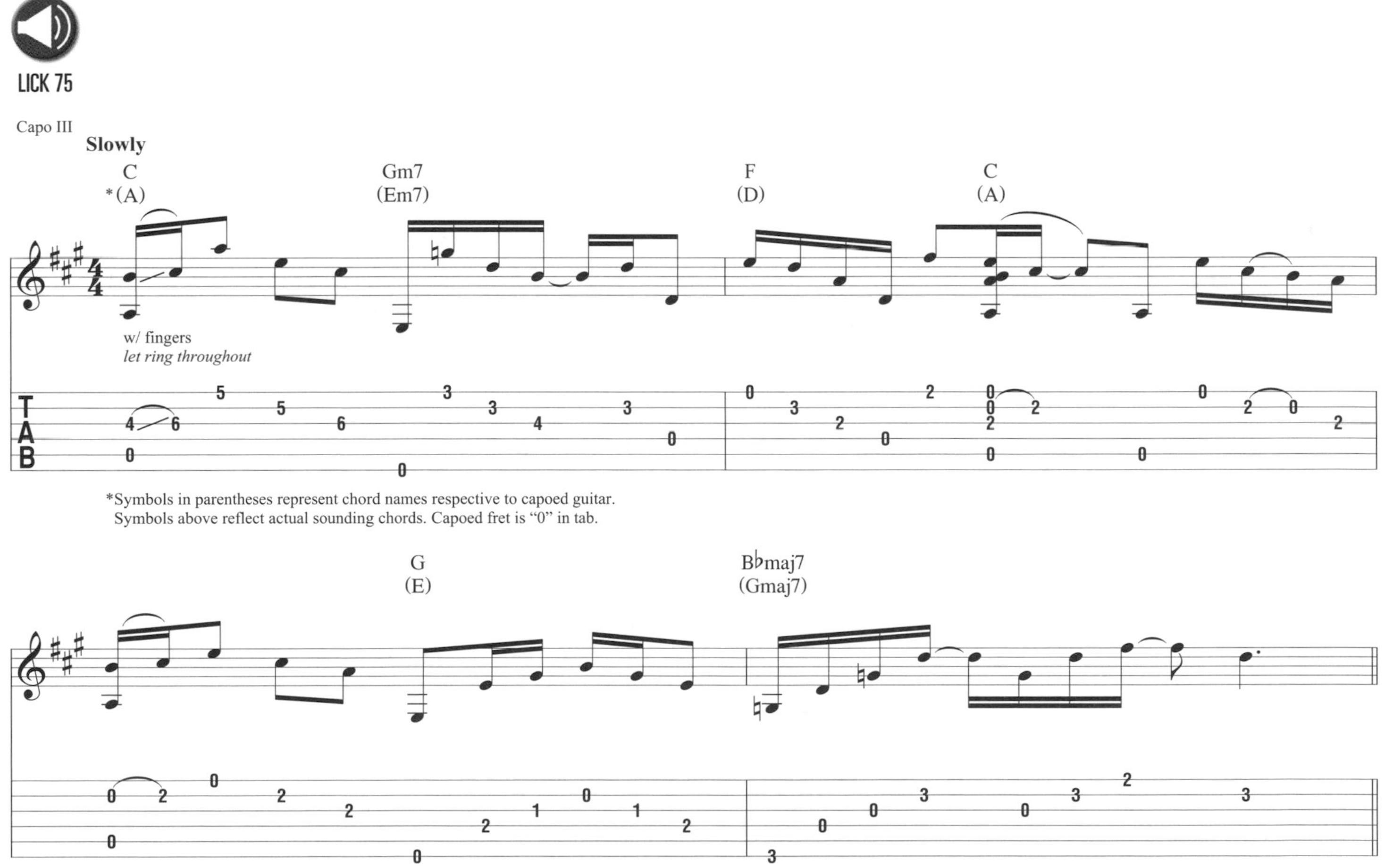

LICK 76

Capo VII

*Symbols in parentheses represent chord names respective to capoed guitar. Symbols above reflect actual sounding chords. Capoed fret is "0" in tab.

LICK 77

Tuning (low to high): E–E↓–E↑–E↓–B–E

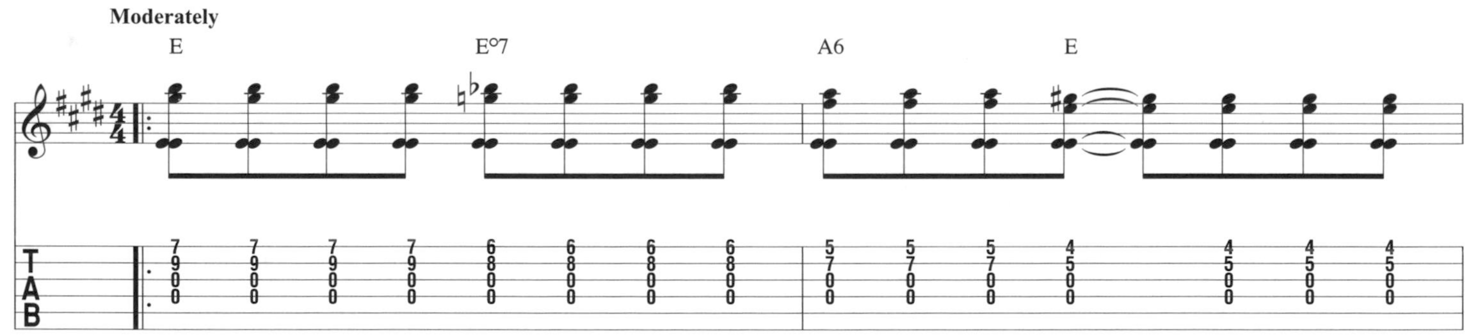

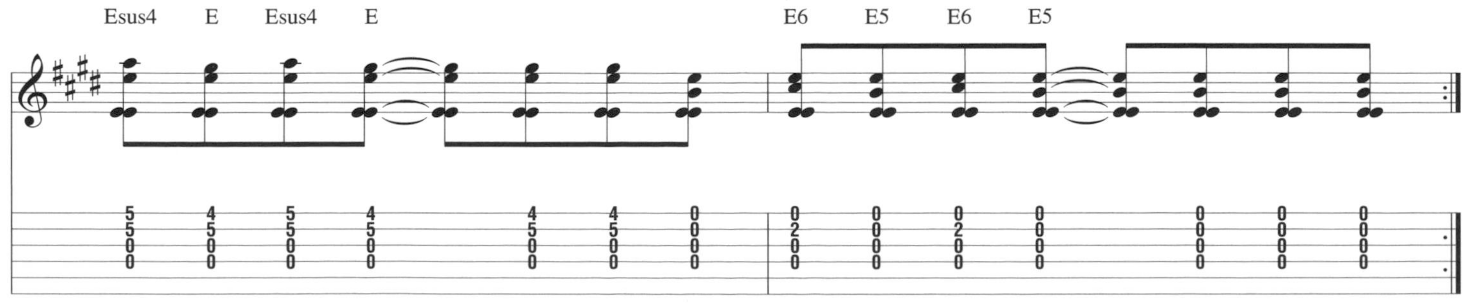

LICK 78

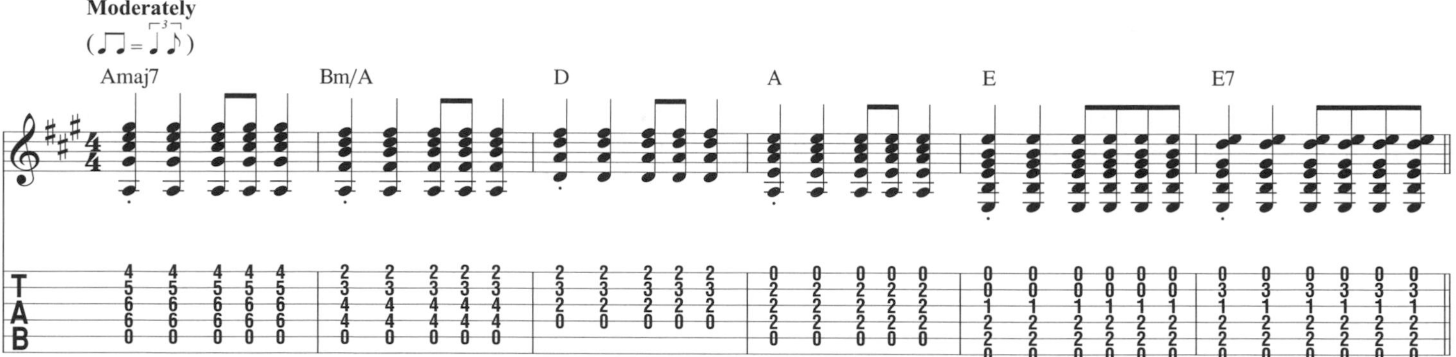

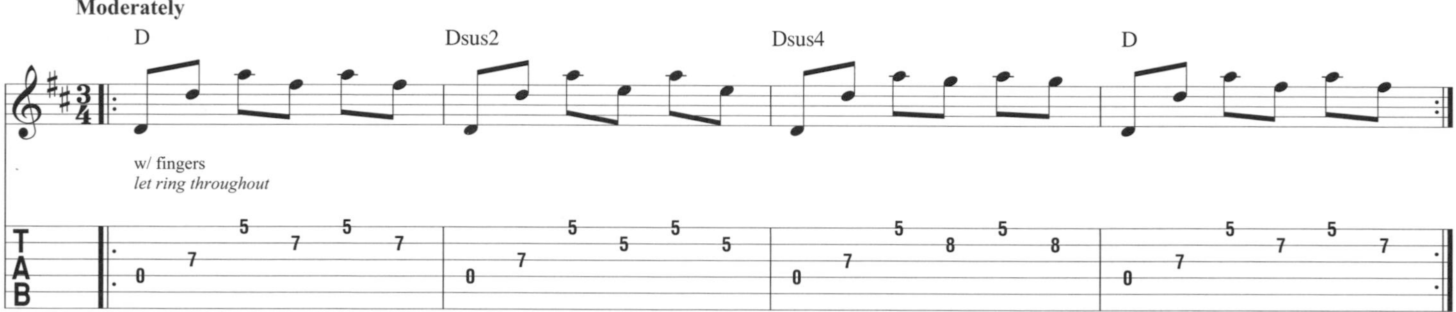

LICK 80

Capo II

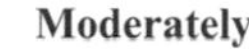

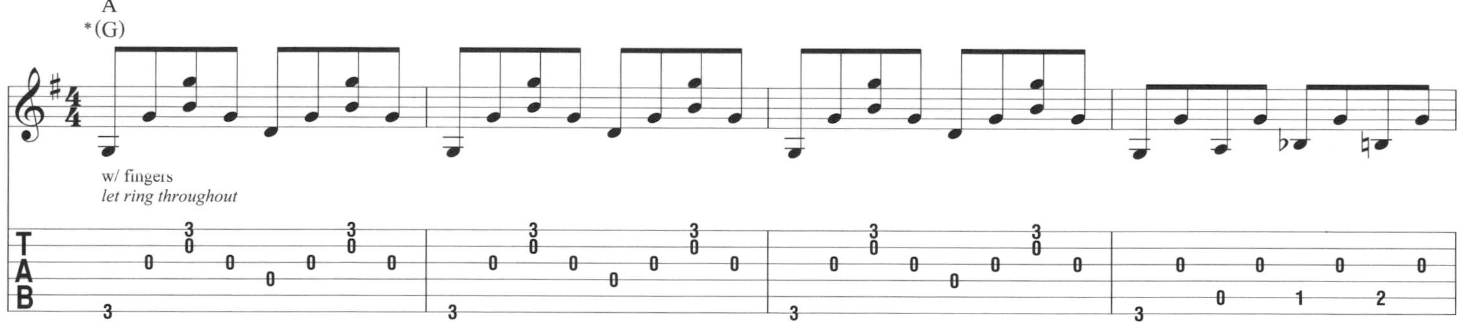

*Symbols in parentheses represent chord names respective to capoed guitar. Symbols above reflect actual sounding chords. Capoed fret is "0" in tab.

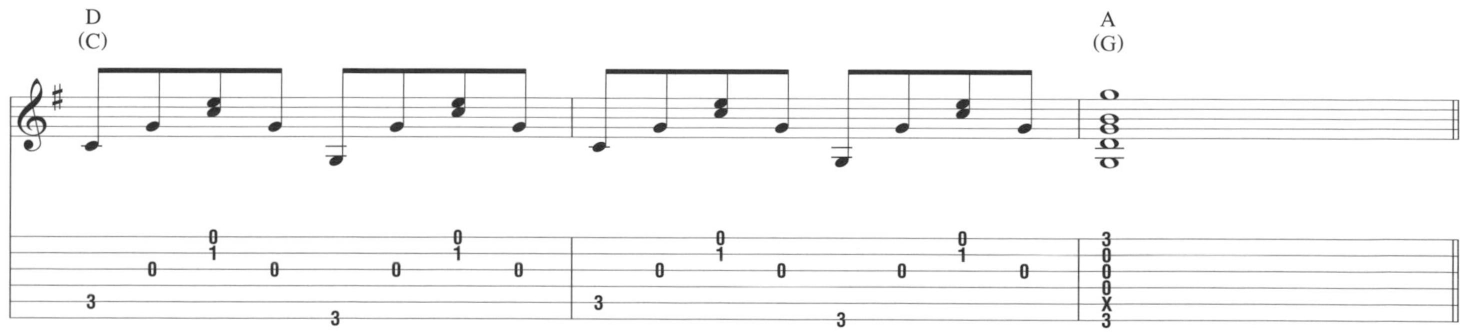

LICK 81

C6 tuning:
(low to high): C–A–C–G–C–E

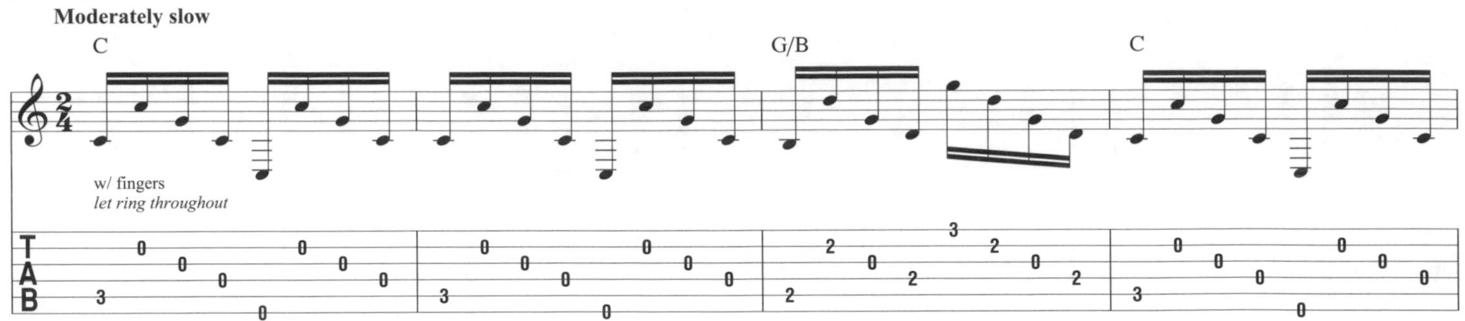

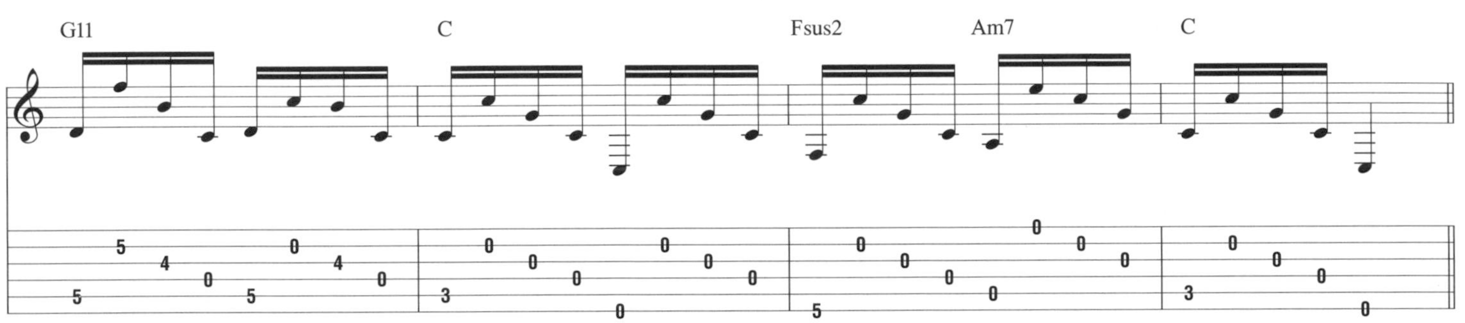

LICK 82

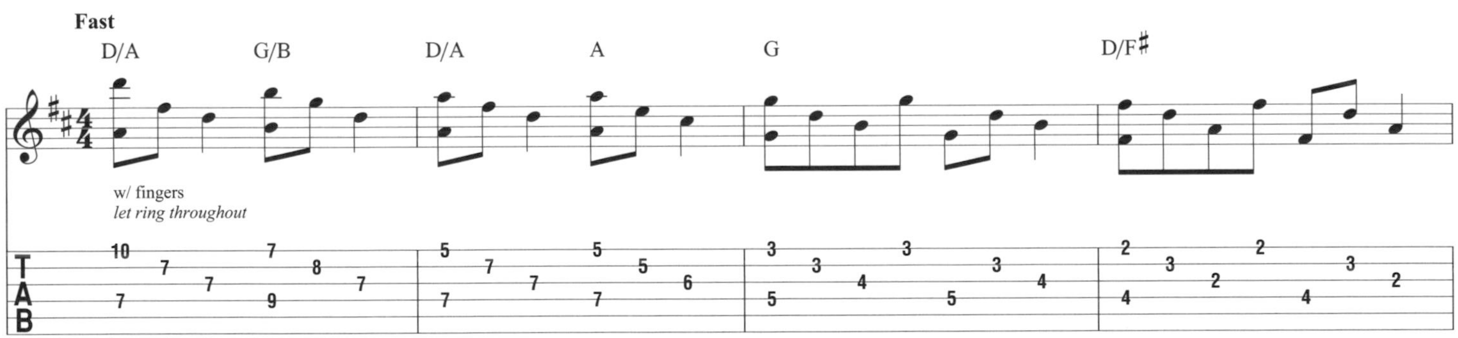

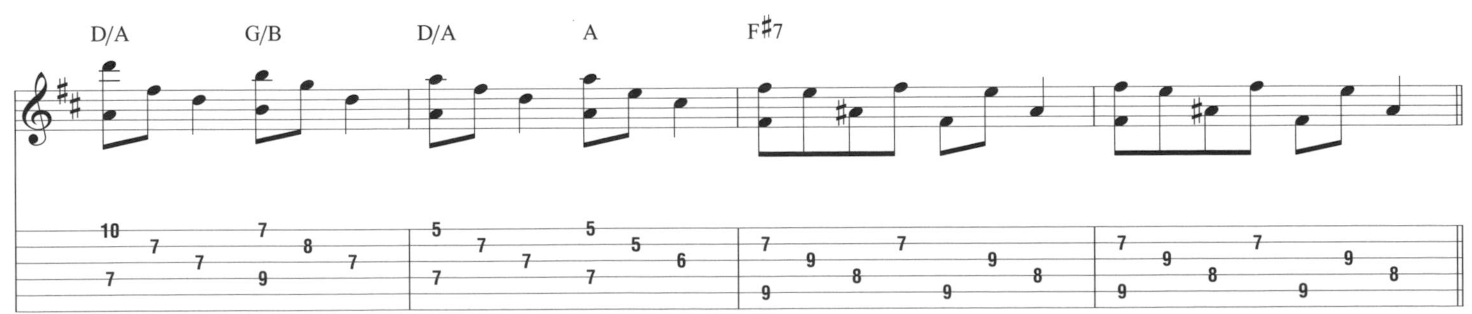

LICK 83

Open E tuning:
(low to high): E–B–E–G♯–B–E

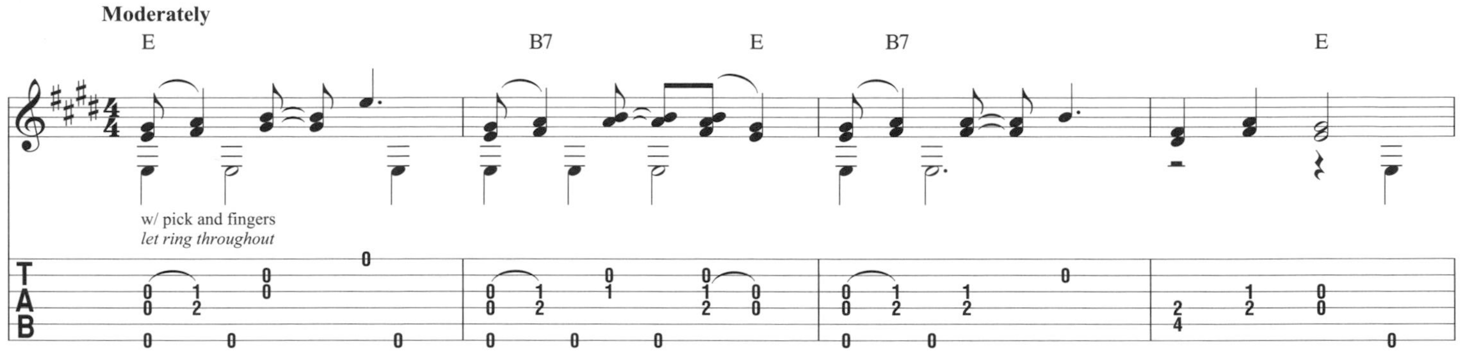

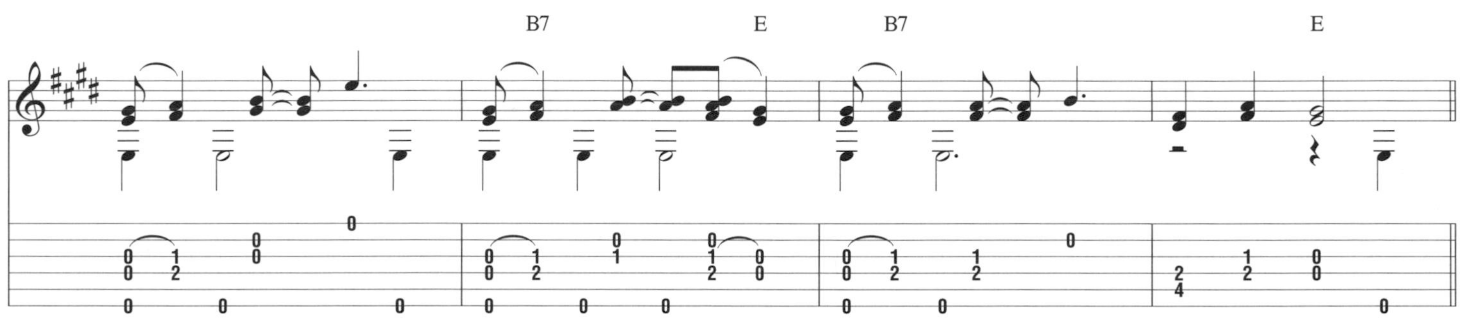

LICK 84

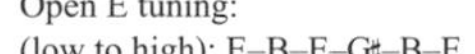

Open E tuning:
(low to high): E–B–E–G♯–B–E

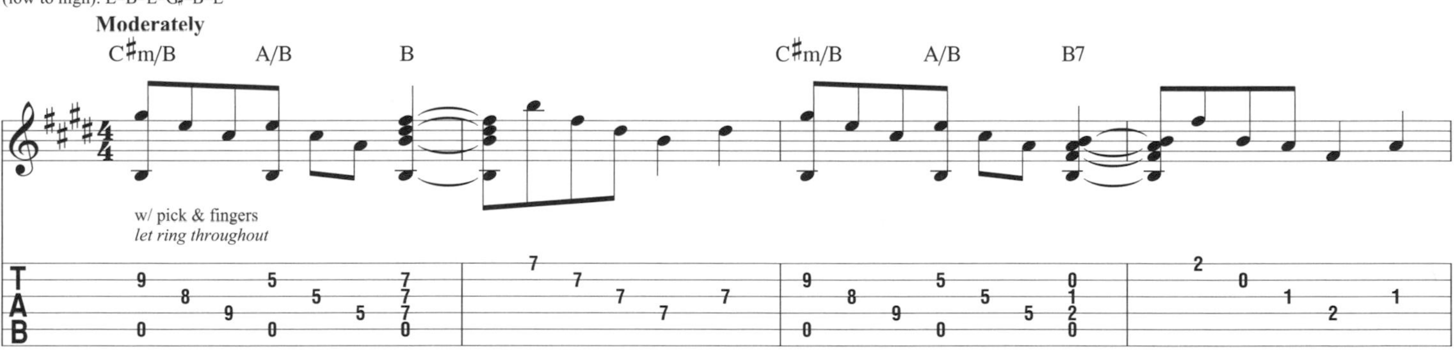

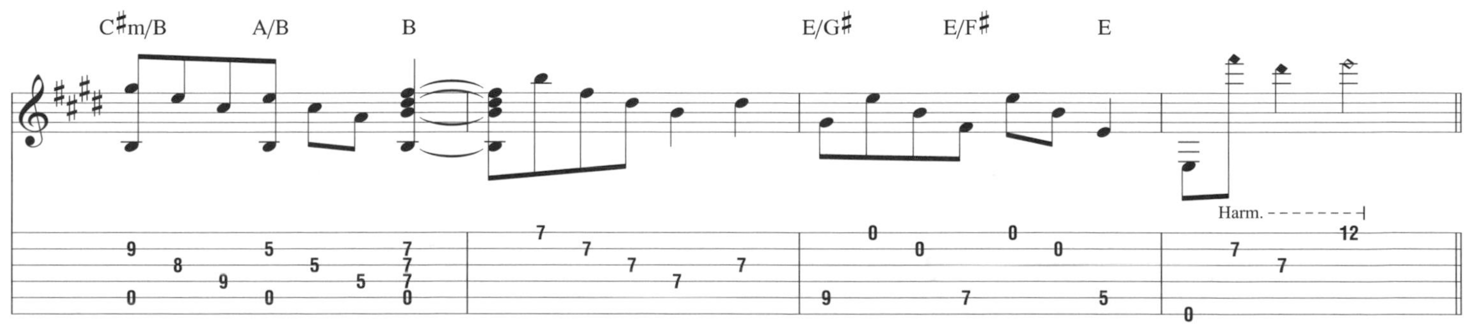

Jazz

Jazz is renowned for its adventurous soloists and accomplished rhythm players, and that includes its acoustic guitar stylists. The acoustic guitar has figured prominently in the jazz genre since the late '20s, when it replaced the banjo as the instrument of choice in the rhythm section of big bands and studio orchestras. Early masters include Eddie Lang, Carl Kress, Dick McDonough, Lonnie Johnson, Nick Lucas, and the innovative George Van Eps. However, none of these potent players affected the guitar world like its first acoustic jazz virtuoso: Django Reinhardt.

Django Reinhardt is the father of Gypsy jazz, a subgenre enjoying a strong popular revival in recent years. Back in the '30s, Django breathed fire and brought an exotic European flair to the swing style of the period. He also defied and transcended the limitations of a tremendous physical disability: his burned and mutilated fretting hand. Django has been cited as a role model for players as diverse as Johnny Smith, Chet Atkins, Steve Howe, Tommy Tedesco, Joe Pass, Peter Frampton, Biréli Lagrène, and John Jorgenson. He elevated the art of acoustic jazz guitar technique with complex single-note phrases, soulful embellishments, and even some pre-Wes Montgomery octave playing.

The acoustic guitar as a soloist's instrument in jazz took a back seat to its electric counterpart following the Charlie Christian era of the early '40s. Nonetheless, an acoustic instrument in several forms remained a vital tool in the jazz guitarist's arsenal. The nylon-string acoustic played an important role in Antônio Carlos Jobim's bossa nova compositions, other Latin and ethnic forms, and with contemporary performers like Earl Klugh, Lee Ritenour, Gene Bertoncini, and Jeff Linsky. Big-band rhythm guitar work has, since its inception, demanded an archtop instrument à la Freddie Green, Steve Jordan, and Allan Reuss. The aforementioned Gypsy jazz revival ignited a new passion for the unique tone of Selmer/Maccaferri style boxes, now crafted by a new generation of luthiers and played by a new generation of virtuosi. And traditional flat-top steel-string acoustics have cropped up regularly in the music of Joe Pass, Al Di Meola, and Kenny Burrell.

LICK 85

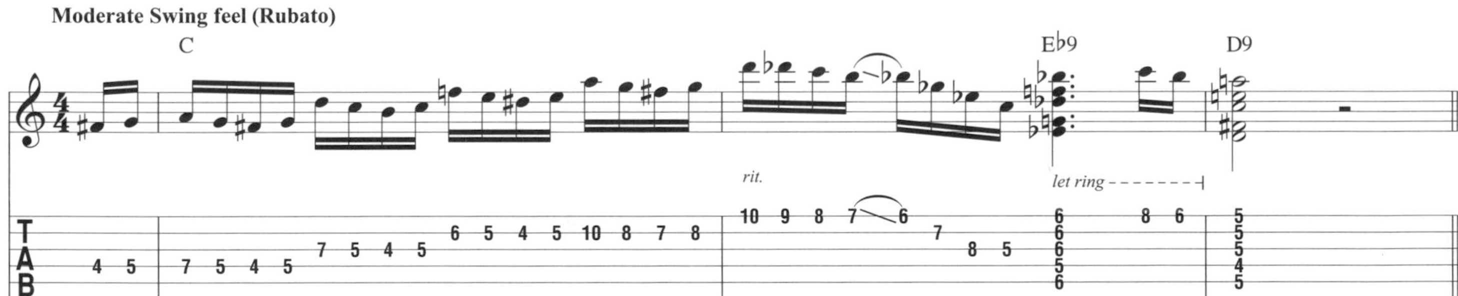

LICK 86

LICK 87

Moderate Swing

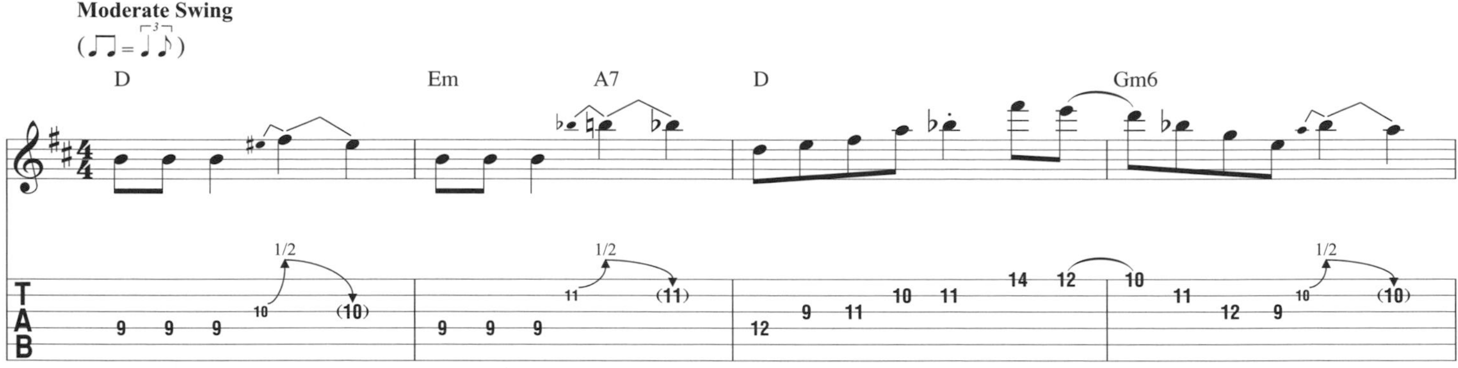

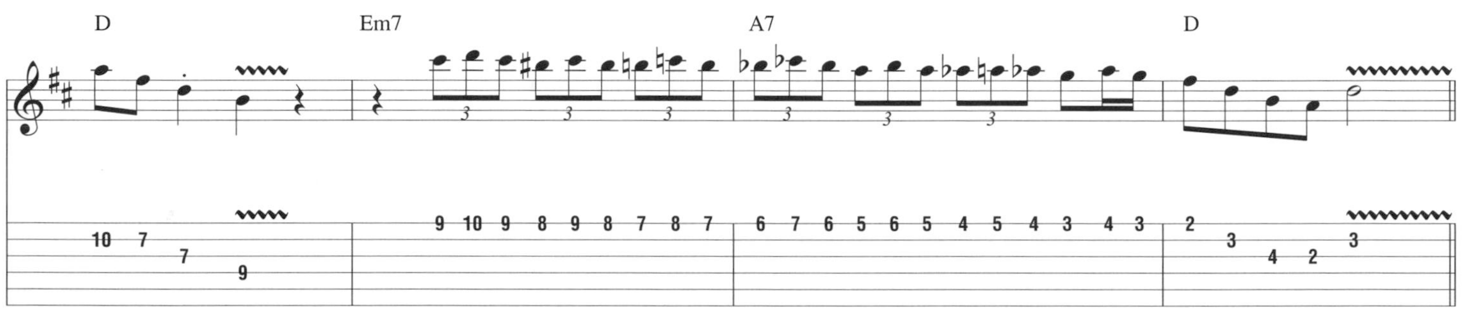

LICK 88

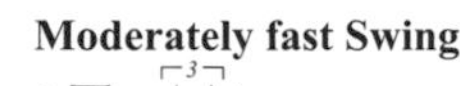

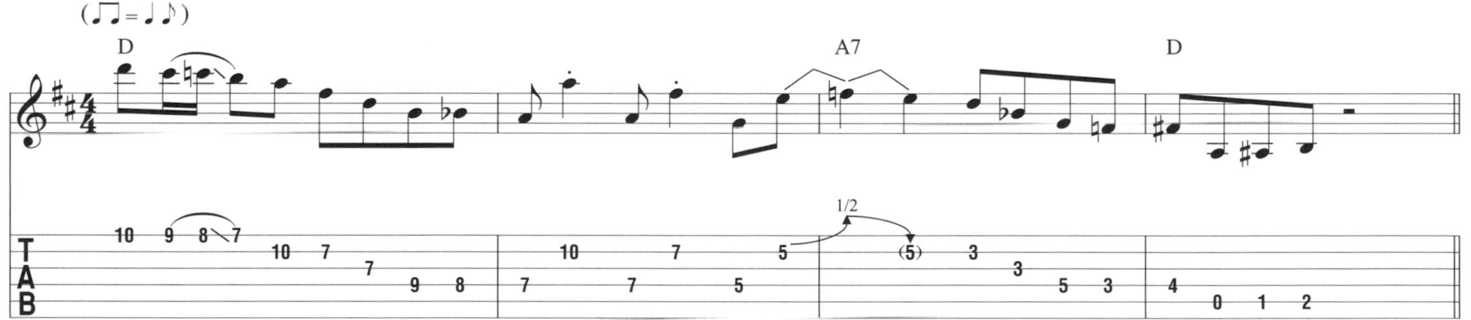

LICK 89

LICK 90

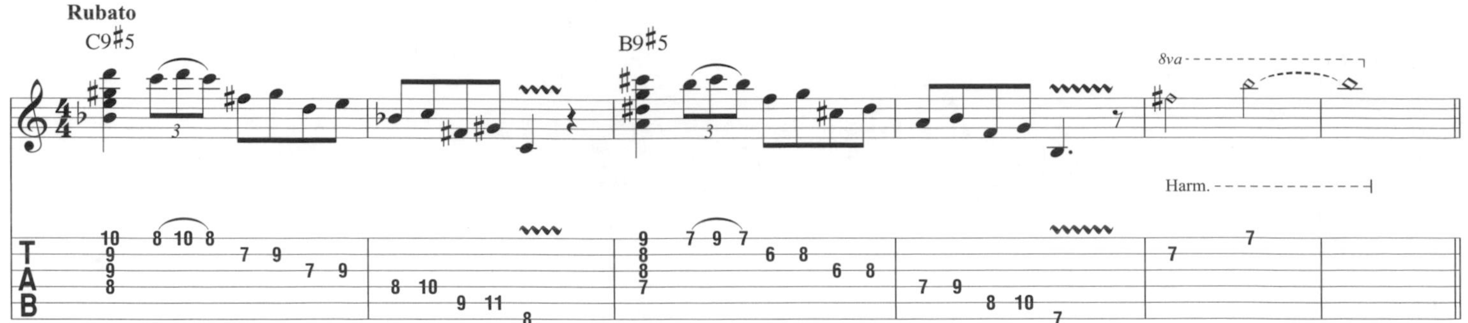

LICK 91

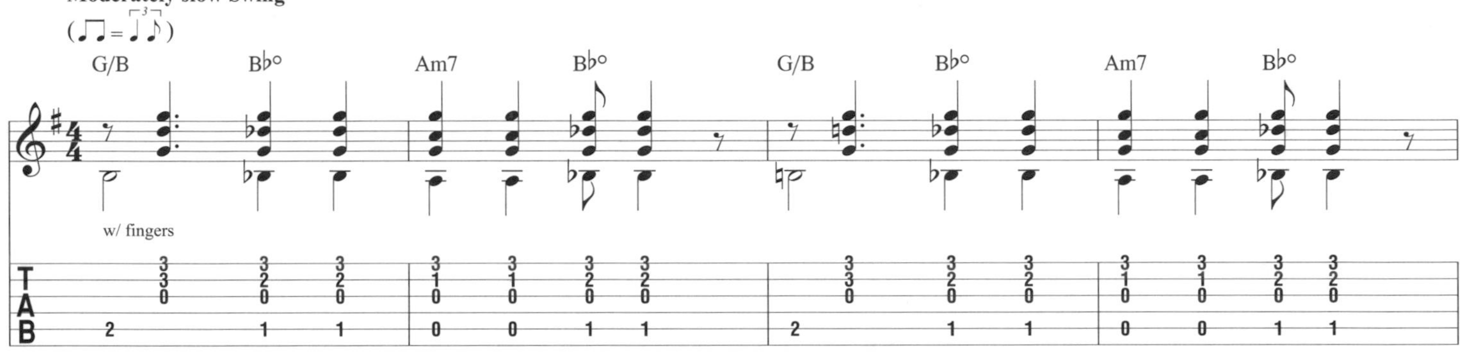

LICK 92

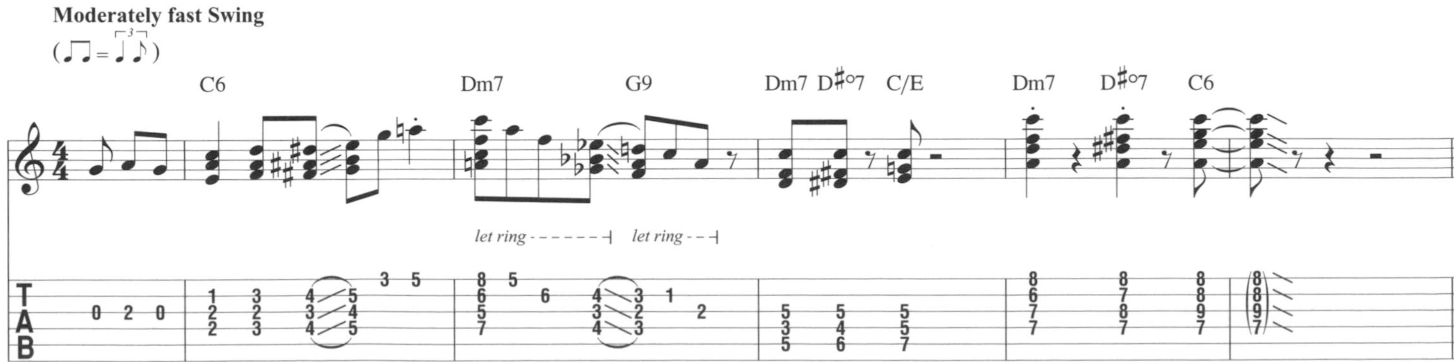

LICK 93

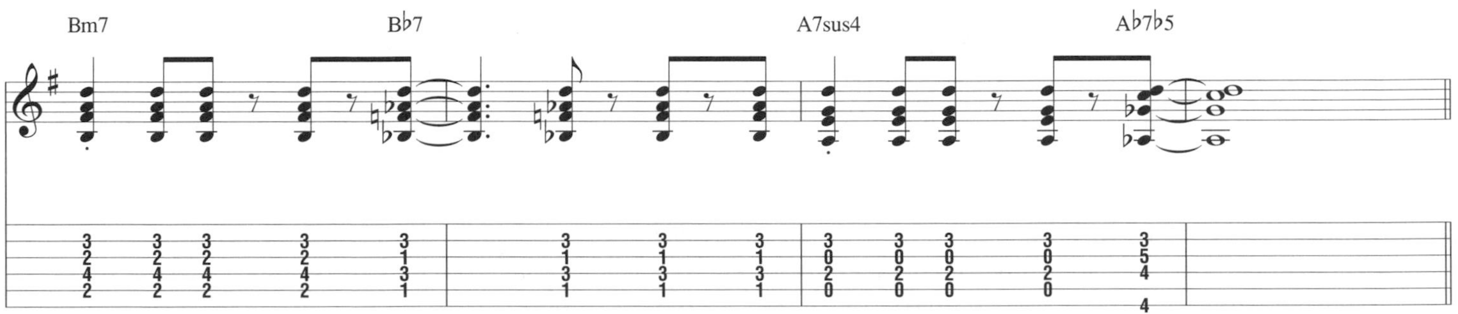

LICK 94

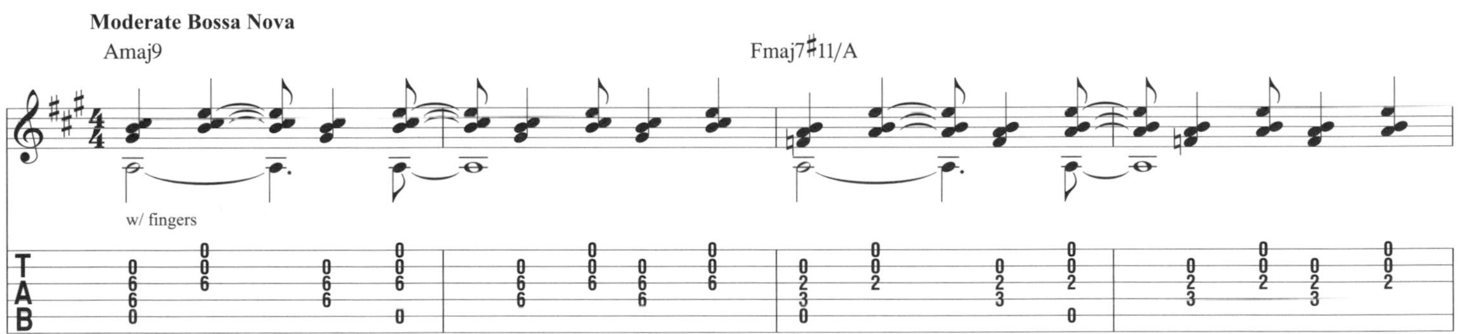

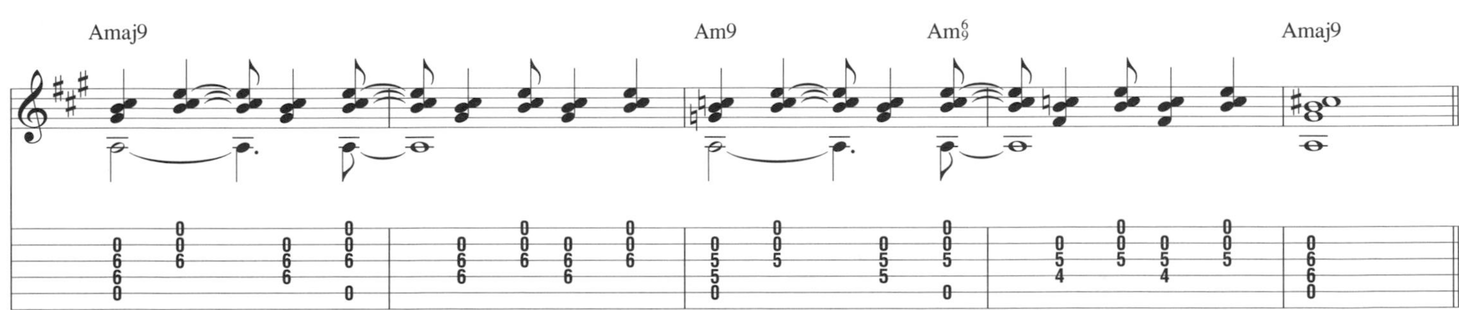

Country

Not that long ago, the only kind of guitar welcomed at the Grand Ole Opry of Nashville, the world's leading country venue, was the unplugged variety. And while that's changed through the efforts of Chet Atkins, Merle Travis, Hank Garland, Albert Lee, Brad Paisley, and a host of other important plugged-in pickers, the acoustic guitar remains an indispensable voice in country music.

Historically, country guitar evolved from bluegrass, Appalachian folk music, and Anglo-American string-band traditions. Bluegrass was enriched at the outset through its transplanted fiddle tunes and chanteys, invariably accompanied by powerful background parts on strummed acoustic guitars. Bluegrass guitar led pickers to emulate intricate fiddle lines early on and laid the foundation for the modern school of country pickin', which is now largely an electric medium.

When country music established its hegemony with a mass audience in the '40s and '50s, the acoustic guitar also increased in stature. It was seen regularly in the hands of its foremost artists, including strummers such as Hank Williams, Jim Reeves, and Gene Autry. Country music and acoustic guitar continued and reinforced its strong connection through the work of artists like Jimmie Rodgers, the Carter Family, Merle Travis, Chet Atkins, Jerry Reed, Ricky Skaggs, and many others.

The first wave of rockabilly artists in the '50s, raised with country and hillbilly influences, combined the genre's characteristic rhythms with swing jazz, blues, and R&B material—and naturally appropriated the role of the acoustic guitar. Notable stars like Elvis Presley, the Everly Brothers, Johnny Cash, Rick Nelson, Gene Vincent, and Roy Orbison fronted their seminal outfits sporting acoustic guitars and country mannerisms.

As rock music evolved in the mid-'60s, it borrowed, unabashedly, from its country cousin. The Beatles plainly alluded to country music with acoustic timbres and stylistic gestures, as did Steve Howe of the progressive rock supergroup Yes. Similar crossover moments are found in the repertories of Rik Emmett, Steve Morse, and other skilled rock pickers bearing a country influence.

LICK 95

Moderate fast Country Swing

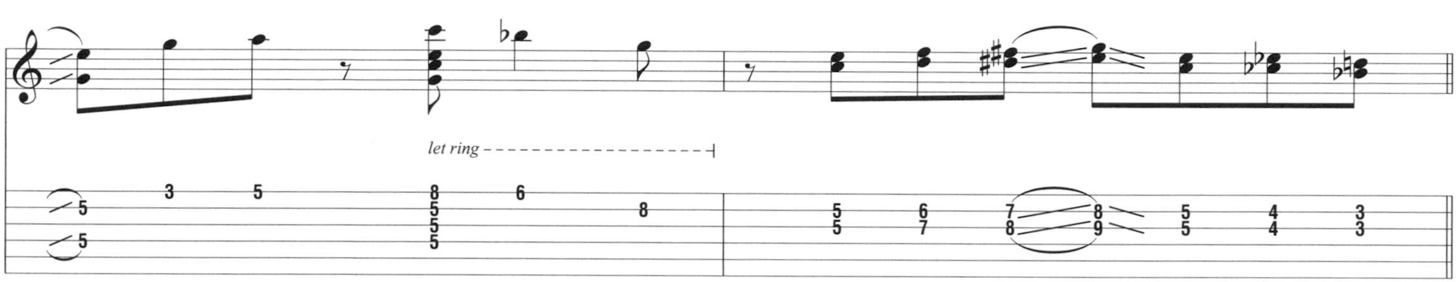

LICK 97

Moderately fast Country Rag

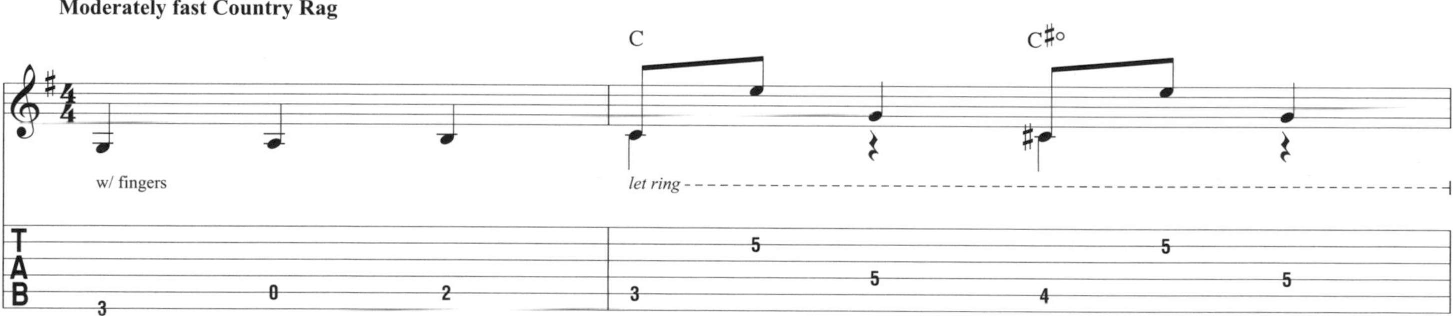

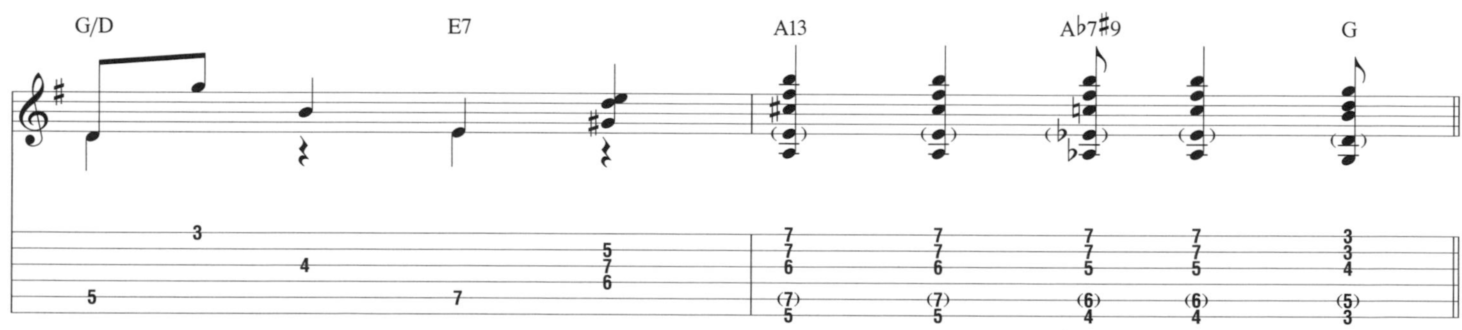

LICK 98

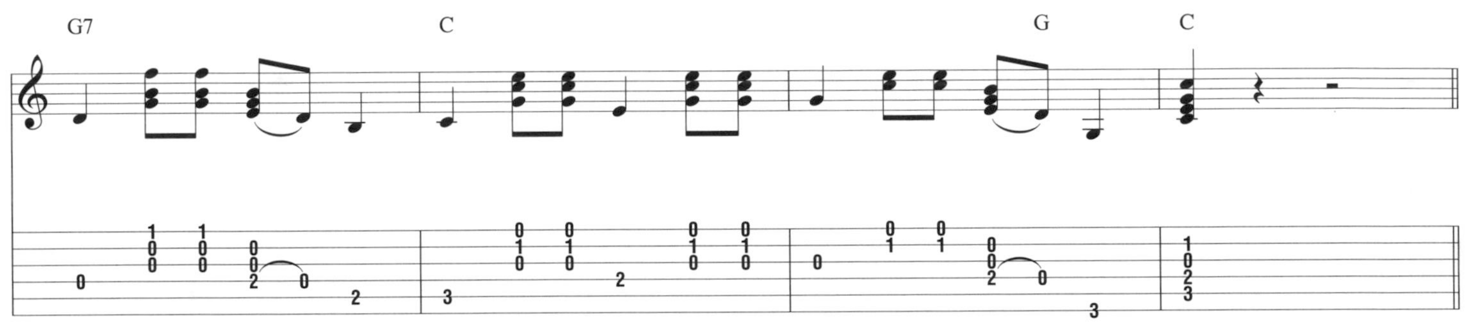

LICK 99

LICK 100

Moderately fast Country Swing

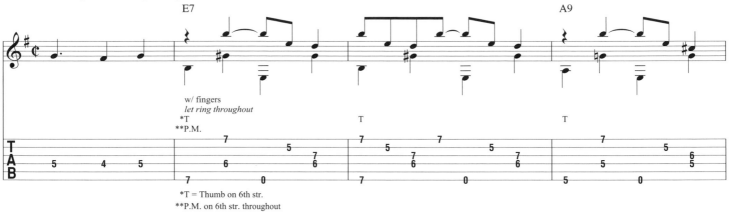

*T = Thumb on 6th str.
**P.M. on 6th str. throughout

LICK 101

Moderately fast Country Rag

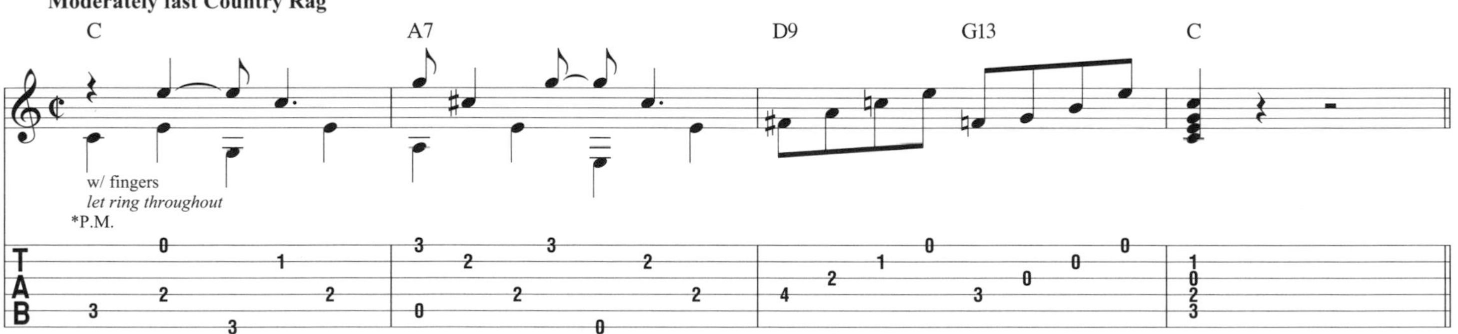

*P.M. on 6th and 5th strings throughout.

Suggested Recordings

Studying music is a lifelong commitment. If you wish to investigate the wonders of the unplugged world more thoroughly, here are some definitive guitar recordings filled with must-know licks offered for your continuing exploration and appreciation.

Classical

Andrés Segovia: *The Segovia Collection* (Deutsche Grammophon)

Julian Bream: *Fret Works* (MCA)

Christopher Parkening: *The Artistry of Christopher Parkening* (EMI Classics)

Blues

Robert Johnson: *King of the Delta Blues Singers* (Columbia)

Skip James: *The Very Best of Skip James* (Fuel 2000)

Lightnin' Hopkins: *The Very Best of Lightnin' Hopkins* (Rykodisc)

Eric Clapton: *Eric Clapton Unplugged* (Warner Bros.)

Pop and Rock

Elvis Presley: *The Sun Sessions* (RCA Victor)

The Everly Brothers: *Cadence Classics* (Rhino)

The Beatles: *Rubber Soul* (Apple)
Beatles (White Album) (Apple)
Abbey Road (Apple)

The Who: *Who's Better, Who's Best* (MCA)

Simon & Garfunkel: *Bookends* (Columbia)

Led Zeppelin: *Led Zeppelin Box Set 1 and 2* (Atlantic)

Steve Morse: *High Tension Wires* (MCA)

Yes: *The Yes Album* (Atlantic)
Fragile (Atlantic)

Kansas:	*The Best of Kansas* (CBS Associated Legacy/Epic)
Boston:	*Greatest Hits* (Epic)
Jim Croce:	*Classic Hits* (Rhino)
Allman Brothers Band:	*A Decade of Hits 1969–1979* (Polydor)
Eagles:	*Their Greatest Hits (1971–1975)* (Asylum) *Eagles Greatest Hits (Vol. 2)* (Asylum)
Van Halen:	*Van Halen II* (Warner Bros.) *Women and Children First* (Warner Bros.)
Randy Rhoads:	Ozzy Osbourne: *Blizzard of Ozz* (Jet) Ozzy Osbourne: *Diary of a Madman* (Jet)
Yngwie Malmsteen:	*Rising Force* (Polydor)
Bon Jovi:	*Cross Road* (Mercury, Polygram)
Metallica:	*Metallica (Black Album)* (Elektra)
Sheryl Crow:	*The Very Best of Sheryl Crow* (A&M)
Dave Matthews:	*Under the Table and Dreaming* (RCA) *The Best of What's Around (Vol. I)* (RCA)
John Mayer:	*Continuum* (Columbia, Aware)

Folk

Peter, Paul & Mary:	*The Very Best of Peter, Paul & Mary* (Rhino)
Kingston Trio:	*The Essential Kingston Trio* (Shout Factory)
Bob Dylan:	*The Freewheelin' Bob Dylan* (Columbia) *The Times They Are A-Changin'* (Columbia) *Bob Dylan's Greatest Hits* (Columbia)
Crosby, Stills & Nash:	*Crosby, Stills & Nash* (Atlantic)
James Taylor:	*Greatest Hits* (Warner Bros.)
Joni Mitchell:	*Ladies of the Canyon* (Reprise)
John Denver:	*John Denver's Greatest Hits* (RCA)

Jazz

Django Reinhardt:	*Verve Jazz Masters 38* (Polygram) *The Complete Django Reinhardt and Quintet of the Hot Club of France Swing/HMV Sessions 1936–1948* (Mosaic) *Djangology* (Bluebird)
Various:	*Pioneers of the Jazz Guitar* (Yazoo)
Freddie Green:	*The Complete Atomic Basie* (Roulette)
Antônio C. Jobim:	*The Composer of Desafinado Plays* (Verve)
Kenny Burrell:	*Guitar Forms* (Verve)
Joe Pass:	*Virtuoso* (Pablo)
Earl Klugh:	*The Best of Earl Klugh* (Warner Bros.)
Al Di Meola:	*Friday Night in San Francisco* (Philips)
John McLaughlin:	*Shakti* (Columbia)
Biréli Lagrène:	*Gypsy Project* (Dreyfus)
John Jorgenson:	*Franco-American Swing* (Pharaoh)

Country

Jimmie Rodgers:	*The Essential Jimmie Rodgers* (RCA)
The Carter Family:	*The Carter Family Volume 1: 1927–1934* (JSP)
Merle Travis:	*Guitar Retrospective* (CMH)
Chet Atkins:	*Legendary* (BMG Int'l)
Jerry Reed:	*The Essential Jerry Reed* (RCA)
Doyle Dykes:	*Fingerstyle Guitar* (Step One)
Tommy Emmanuel:	*Center Stage* (Favored Nations)

GUITAR NOTATION LEGEND

Guitar music can be notated three different ways: on a *musical staff*, in *tablature*, and in *rhythm slashes*.

RHYTHM SLASHES are written above the staff. Strum chords in the rhythm indicated. Use the chord diagrams found at the top of the first page of the transcription for the appropriate chord voicings. Round noteheads indicate single notes.

THE MUSICAL STAFF shows pitches and rhythms and is divided by bar lines into measures. Pitches are named after the first seven letters of the alphabet.

TABLATURE graphically represents the guitar fingerboard. Each horizontal line represents a string, and each number represents a fret.

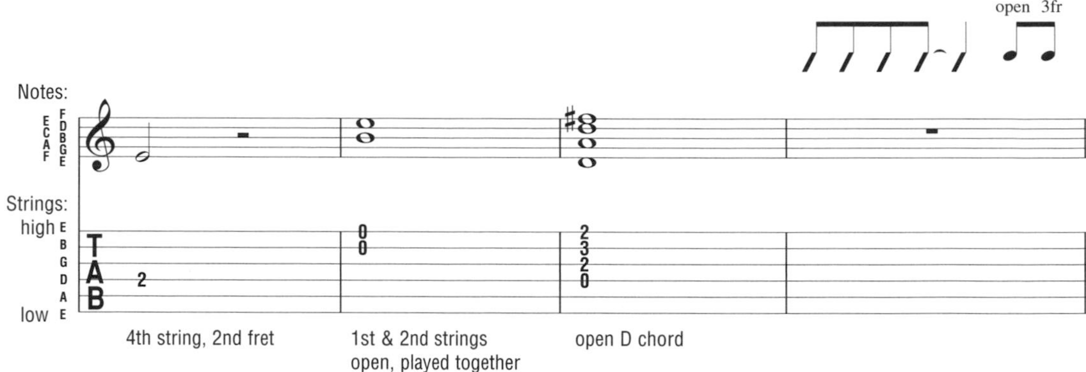

4th string, 2nd fret

1st & 2nd strings open, played together

open D chord

Definitions for Special Guitar Notation

HALF-STEP BEND: Strike the note and bend up 1/2 step.

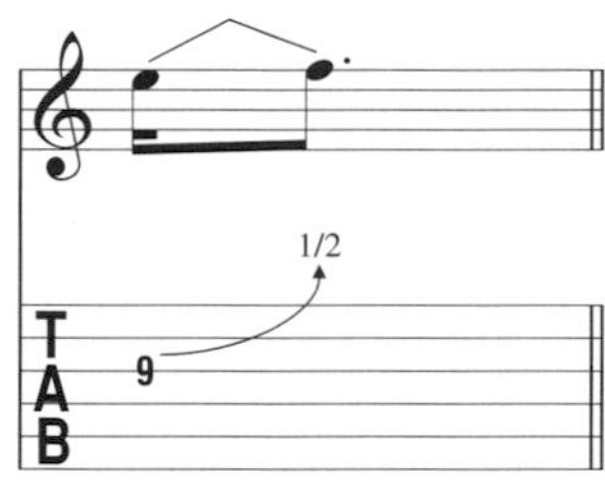

WHOLE-STEP BEND: Strike the note and bend up one step.

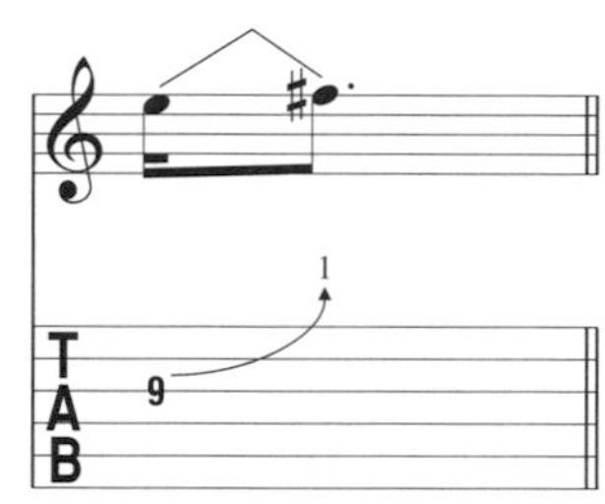

GRACE NOTE BEND: Strike the note and immediately bend up as indicated.

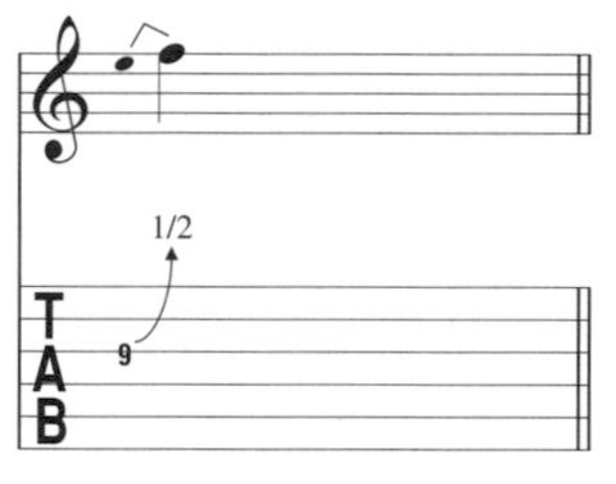

SLIGHT (MICROTONE) BEND: Strike the note and bend up 1/4 step.

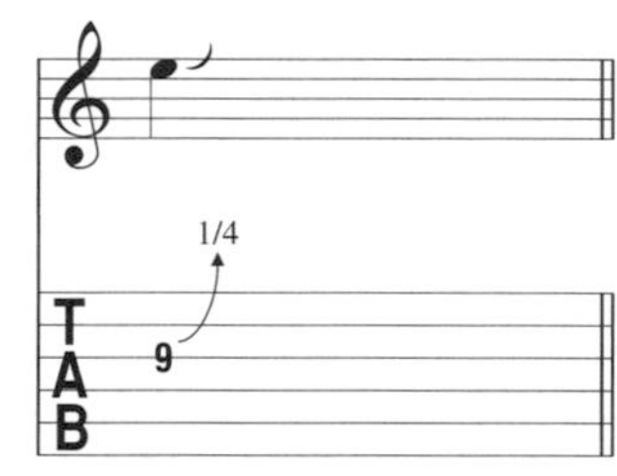

BEND AND RELEASE: Strike the note and bend up as indicated, then release back to the original note. Only the first note is struck.

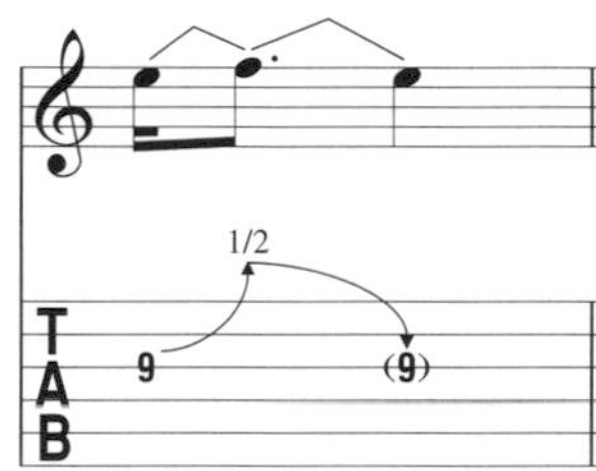
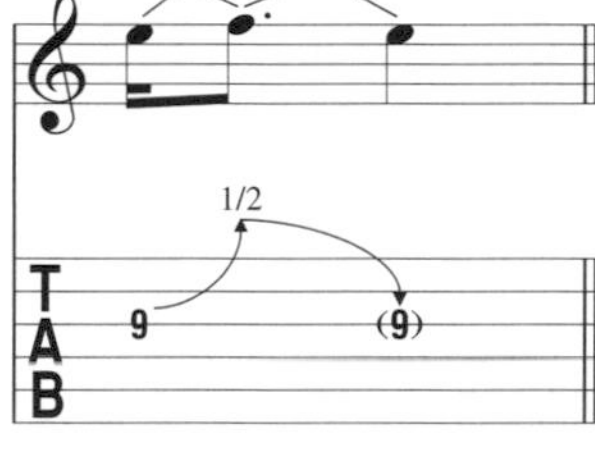

PRE-BEND: Bend the note as indicated, then strike it.

PRE-BEND AND RELEASE: Bend the note as indicated. Strike it and release the bend back to the original note.

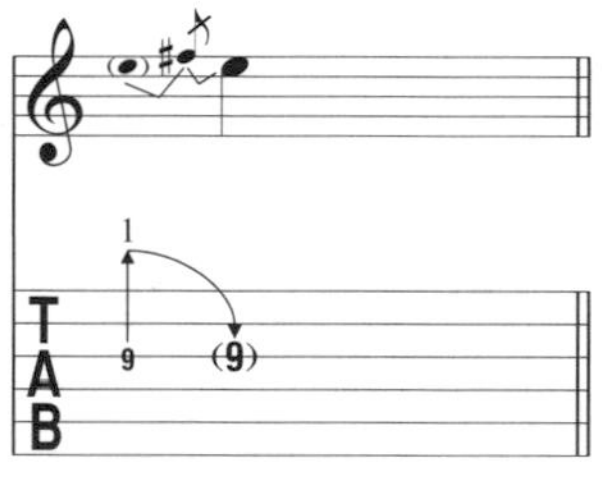

UNISON BEND: Strike the two notes simultaneously and bend the lower note up to the pitch of the higher.

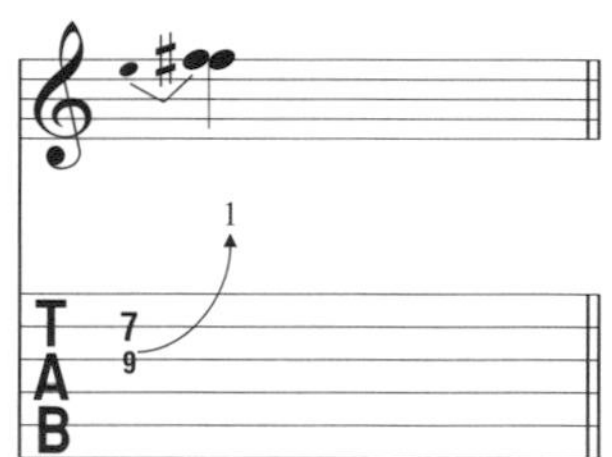

VIBRATO: The string is vibrated by rapidly bending and releasing the note with the fretting hand.

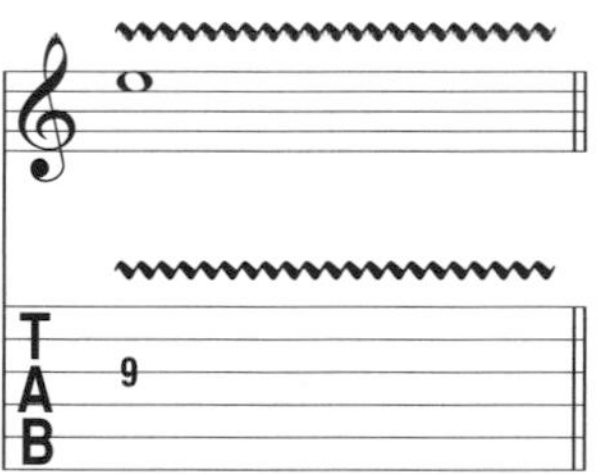

WIDE VIBRATO: The pitch is varied to a greater degree by vibrating with the fretting hand.

HAMMER-ON: Strike the first (lower) note with one finger, then sound the higher note (on the same string) with another finger by fretting it without picking.

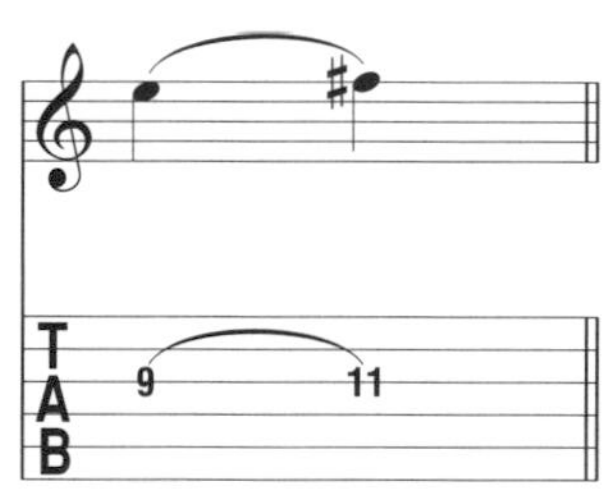

PULL-OFF: Place both fingers on the notes to be sounded. Strike the first note and without picking, pull the finger off to sound the second (lower) note.

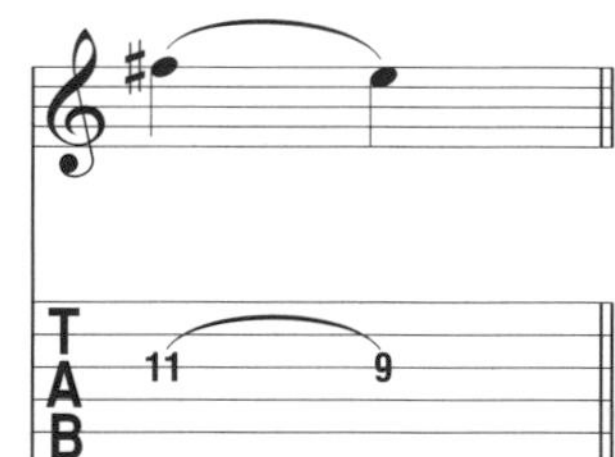

LEGATO SLIDE: Strike the first note and then slide the same fret-hand finger up or down to the second note. The second note is not struck.

SHIFT SLIDE: Same as legato slide, except the second note is struck.

TRILL: Very rapidly alternate between the notes indicated by continuously hammering on and pulling off.

TAPPING: Hammer ("tap") the fret indicated with the pick-hand index or middle finger and pull off to the note fretted by the fret hand.

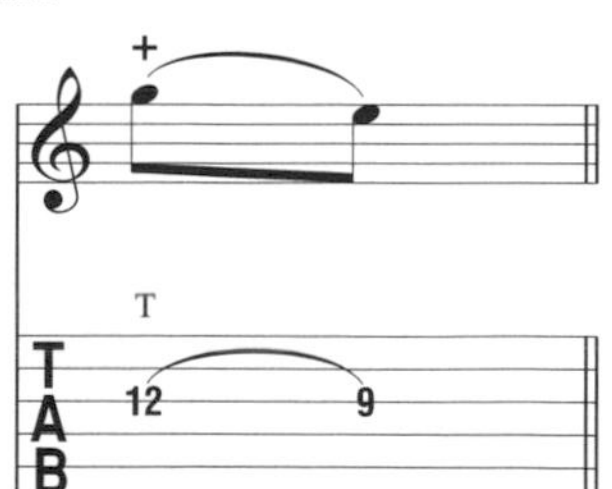

NATURAL HARMONIC: Strike the note while the fret-hand lightly touches the string directly over the fret indicated.

PINCH HARMONIC: The note is fretted normally and a harmonic is produced by adding the edge of the thumb or the tip of the index finger of the pick hand to the normal pick attack.

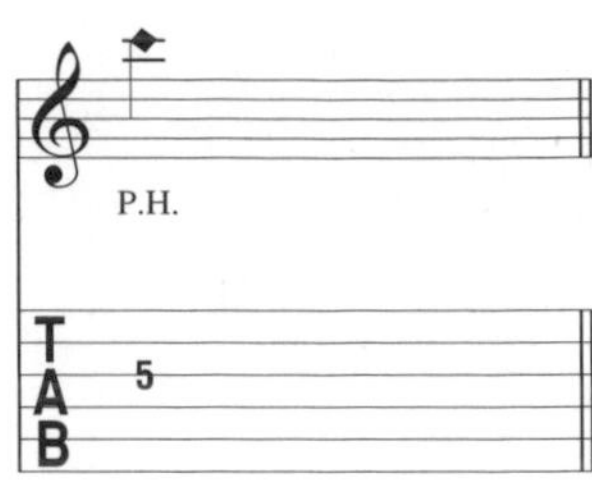

HARP HARMONIC: The note is fretted normally and a harmonic is produced by gently resting the pick hand's index finger directly above the indicated fret (in parentheses) while the pick hand's thumb or pick assists by plucking the appropriate string.

PICK SCRAPE: The edge of the pick is rubbed down (or up) the string, producing a scratchy sound.

MUFFLED STRINGS: A percussive sound is produced by laying the fret hand across the string(s) without depressing, and striking them with the pick hand.

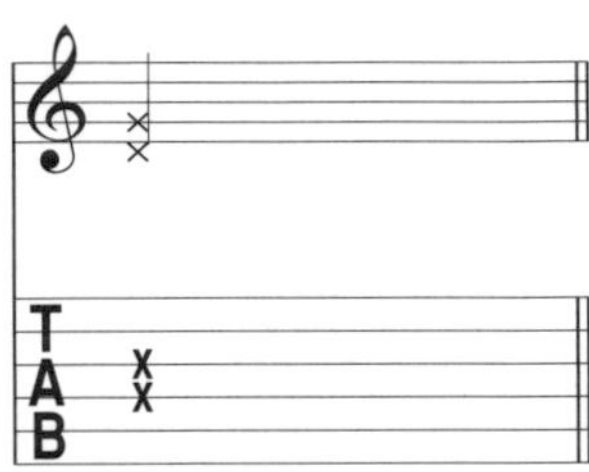

PALM MUTING: The note is partially muted by the pick hand lightly touching the string(s) just before the bridge.

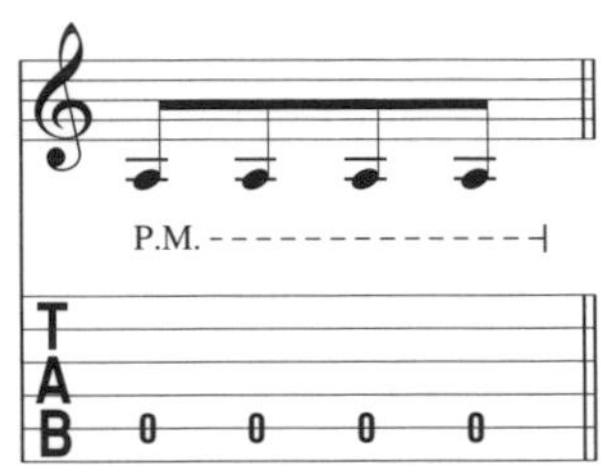

RAKE: Drag the pick across the strings indicated with a single motion.

TREMOLO PICKING: The note is picked as rapidly and continuously as possible.

ARPEGGIATE: Play the notes of the chord indicated by quickly rolling them from bottom to top.

VIBRATO BAR DIVE AND RETURN: The pitch of the note or chord is dropped a specified number of steps (in rhythm), then returned to the original pitch.

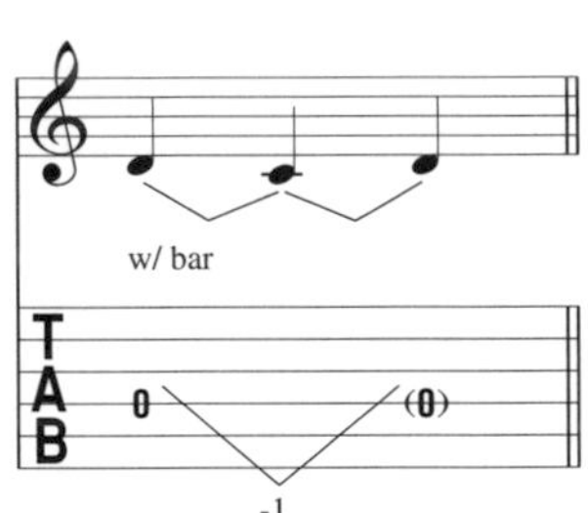

VIBRATO BAR SCOOP: Depress the bar just before striking the note, then quickly release the bar.

VIBRATO BAR DIP: Strike the note and then immediately drop a specified number of steps, then release back to the original pitch.

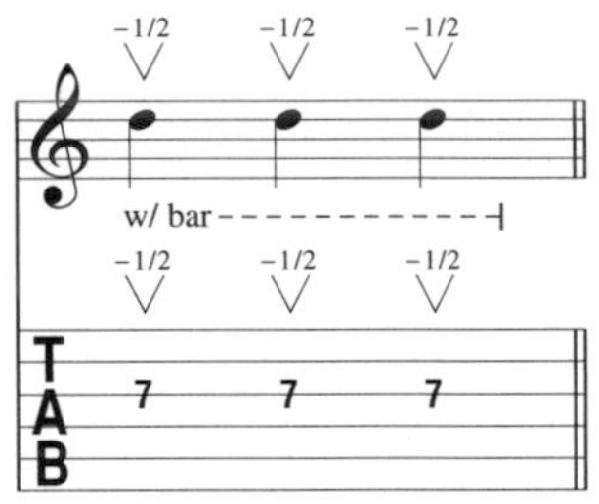

Additional Musical Definitions

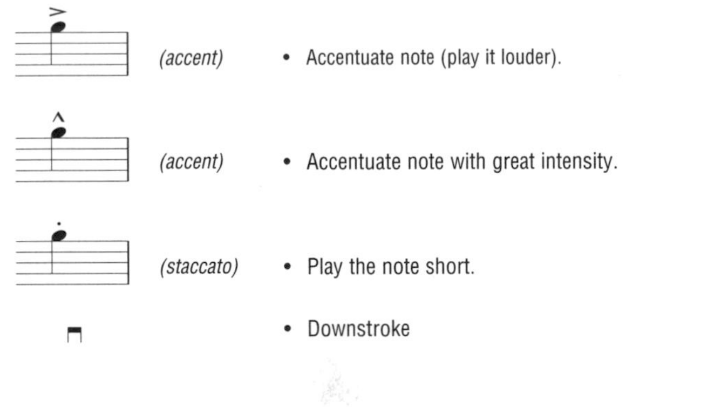

(accent) • Accentuate note (play it louder).

(accent) • Accentuate note with great intensity.

(staccato) • Play the note short.

• Downstroke

• Upstroke

D.S. al Coda • Go back to the sign (𝄋), then play until the measure marked "***To Coda***," then skip to the section labelled "**Coda**."

D.C. al Fine • Go back to the beginning of the song and play until the measure marked "***Fine***" (end).

Rhy. Fig. • Label used to recall a recurring accompaniment pattern (usually chordal).

Riff • Label used to recall composed, melodic lines (usually single notes) which recur.

Fill • Label used to identify a brief melodic figure which is to be inserted into the arrangement.

Rhy. Fill • A chordal version of a Fill.

tacet • Instrument is silent (drops out).

• Repeat measures between signs.

1. 2.

• When a repeated section has different endings, play the first ending only the first time and the second ending only the second time.

NOTE: Tablature numbers in parentheses mean:

1. The note is being sustained over a system (note in standard notation is tied), or
2. The note is sustained, but a new articulation (such as a hammer-on, pull-off, slide or vibrato) begins, or
3. The note is a barely audible "ghost" note (note in standard notation is also in parentheses).